Pre-Intermediate

Student's Book

Part B   Units 8–14

New Headway
English Course

John and Liz Soars

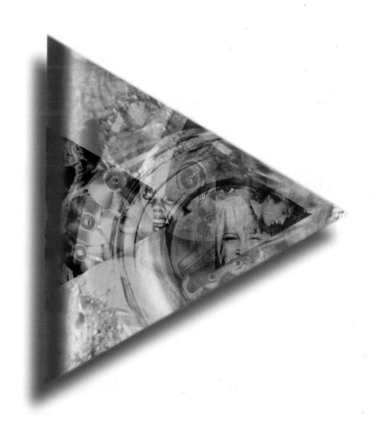

OXFORD
UNIVERSITY PRESS

CONTENTS

SKILLS DEVELOPMENT

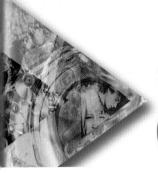

8 Do's and don'ts

have (got) to • *should/must* • Words that go together • At the doctor's

STARTER

What's true for you? Make sentences about your life.

I have to . . .   **I don't have to . . .**
• get up early every morning   • pay bills   • go to school   • work at the weekend   • do the housework

WORK, WORK
have (got) to

1 **T 8.1** Listen to Steven talking about his job. What do you think his job is? Would you like his job? Why/Why not?

2 Complete the sentences from the interview with words from the box.

don't have to   have to   had to   Do you have to   didn't have to

I _____ work very long hours.

_____ work at the weekend?

I _____ do the washing-up.

We _____ learn the basics.

I _____ wait too long to get a job.

3 Change the sentences using *he*.   **He has to work very long hours.**

GRAMMAR SPOT

1 *have/have got* can express possession or an action.
   I **have** my own flat.
   We**'ve got** an exam tomorrow.

2 *have/have got* + infinitive expresses obligation.
   He **has** to work long hours.   I**'ve got** to go now. Bye!

3 Write the question and negative.
   I have to get up early.
   What time ____ you _____ up?
   I _____ up early.
   Put the sentence in the past.
   Yesterday I _____ up early.

▶▶ **Grammar Reference 8.1 p124**

---

4 What are some of the other things Steven has to do?

WHAT'S MY JOB?
STEVEN BARNES

PRACTICE

Pronunciation

1 **T 8.2** Listen to these sentences. What are the different pronunciations of *have/has/had*?

1 ☐ I **have** a good job. ☐ I **have** to work hard.
2 ☐ He **has** a nice car. ☐ She **has** to get up early.
3 ☐ I **had** a good time. ☐ I **had** to take exams.

Put a–f in front of the sentences according to the pronunciation below.

a /hæz/ b /hæv/ c /hæd/
d /hæf/ e /hæs/ f /hæt/

T 8.2 Listen again and repeat.

Jobs

2 Work with a partner. Choose one of the jobs from the box, but don't tell your partner. Ask and answer *Yes/No* questions to find out what the job is.

shop assistant   receptionist   taxi-driver   artist   architect   lawyer
ambulance driver   miner   dancer   soldier   decorator   detective   vet
mechanic   dentist   housewife   farmer   plumber   firefighter

Do you . . . ?
• work inside
• earn a lot of money
• work regular hours

Do you have to . . . ?
• wear a uniform
• use your hands
• answer the phone

Do you work inside?

Yes, I do./No, I don't.

3 Which of the jobs *wouldn't* you like to do? Why?

I wouldn't like to be a farmer because they have to work outside all year.

Talking about you

4 In groups, discuss the questions. If you live at home with your parents, use the present tense. If you've left home, use the past tense.

1 What $\begin{vmatrix} do \\ did \end{vmatrix}$ you have to do to help in the house? What about your brothers and sisters?

2 $\begin{vmatrix} Can \\ Could \end{vmatrix}$ you stay out as long as you $\begin{vmatrix} want? \\ wanted? \end{vmatrix}$ Or $\begin{vmatrix} do \\ did \end{vmatrix}$ you have to be home by a certain time?

3 $\begin{vmatrix} Do \\ Did \end{vmatrix}$ you always have to tell your parents where you $\begin{vmatrix} are \\ were \end{vmatrix}$ going?

4 How strict $\begin{vmatrix} are \\ were \end{vmatrix}$ your parents? What $\begin{vmatrix} do \\ did \end{vmatrix}$ they let you do?

5 What $\begin{vmatrix} do \\ did \end{vmatrix}$ you argue about?

PROBLEMS, PROBLEMS
should, must

1 Match the problems and suggestions on the right. What advice would *you* give?

2 ▶ **T 8.3** Listen and complete the advice. Use the words from the box.

shouldn't	should
must	don't think you should

1 I think you _____ talk to your boss.
2 You _____ drink coffee at night.
3 I _____ go to the wedding.
4 You _____ go to the dentist.

Practise the conversations with a partner.

3 Give advice to your friends.
- I'm overweight.
- I've got exams next week.
- My cat's ill.

- I'm always arguing with my parents.
- It's my parents' wedding anniversary soon.
- My car's making a funny noise.

GRAMMAR SPOT

1 Which sentence expresses a suggestion?
  Which sentence expresses strong obligation?
    You should go on a diet.
    You must go to the doctor's.

2 *Should* and *must* are modal verbs.
    He **must** be careful.
    You **shouldn't** drink and drive.
    What **should** she do?
  Do we add *-s* with *he/she/it*? Do we use *do/does* in the question and negative?

3 We can make a negative suggestion with *I don't think* ...
    I don't think you should smoke so much.

▶▶ **Grammar Reference 8.2–8.4 p124–5**

Problems

I'm working 16 hours a day.

I can't sleep.

My ex-boyfriend's getting married.

I've had a terrible toothache for weeks.

Suggestions

Don't drink coffee at night.

Go to the dentist.

Don't go to the wedding.

Talk to your boss.

PRACTICE

Grammar

1 Make sentences from the chart.

If you want to . . .		
learn English, do well in life, keep fit,	you have to you don't have to you should you shouldn't	work hard. do some sport. learn the grammar. go to university. buy a dictionary. smoke. believe in yourself. speak your language in class.

A trip to your country

2 Someone is coming to stay in your country for six months. What advice can you give?

You should bring warm clothes. **You don't have to get a visa.**
You have to have a passport. **You must try our local speciality.**

Include advice about money, documents, clothes, health, accommodation, and food.

LISTENING AND SPEAKING
Holidays in January

1 Do many people in your country go on holiday in winter? Where do they go? Where would you like to go for a winter holiday? Write a sentence and read it to the class.

I'd like to go to ... because ...

2 **T 8.4** Listen to three people giving advice about visiting their country in the month of January. Complete the chart. Compare your answers with a partner.

	Weather and clothes	Things to do, places to go	Food and drink
Silvia			
Fatima			
Karl			

3 Answer the questions.
1 Which countries are they talking about? How do you know?
2 Look at the photographs. Which country do they go with?
3 Who talked about sport? Which sport?
4 Who talked about money? What did he/she say?
5 Who suggested going on a boat trip? Where?
6 Which of these countries would you like to visit in January? Why?

Speaking

4 Put the words in the correct order to make questions.
1 weather / is / like / in / what / the / January?
2 take / clothes / what / should / I?
3 can / things / sort / of / what / do / I?
4 special / any / there / places / are / that / should / visit / I?
5 food / you / recommend / do / what?

5 Work with someone from a different country, or choose another country you know. Ask and answer the questions.

1 These problems come from a newspaper column where people write in with a problem, and other members of the public give their advice. Read the problems. What advice would you give?

2 Match the readers' letters to these problems. There are two for each problem.

DILEMMAS

with **Vanessa Goodman**

THIS WEEK'S PROBLEMS

Do I have to act my age?

Polly is 47. She is single, and her children have left home. She is very successful in her career, and has a lot of friends, but she isn't satisfied. She longs to change her life. She wants to live abroad, paint, and write poetry, but her friends tell her she should stop being silly and act her age.

a ☐ ☐

Must I be a slave to my mobile?

Jason's company has bought him a mobile phone. They want him to keep it on all the time, so that they can contact him anywhere, anytime. He dislikes the idea of always being available, and he hates the way people use mobiles to have private conversations in public.

b ☐ ☐

Should I throw my son out?

Sarah's 24-year-old son lives at home, stays in bed till late, and watches TV all day. He buys and sells drugs. He's clever, but he dropped out of school. He's never had a job. His father wants to throw him out, but Sarah worries that he could get further into drugs and end up in prison.

c ☐ ☐

READERS' ADVICE

1 Children always need the support of their parents, whether they're four or 24. I think you should pay for him to get some qualifications, and when he's ready, _____ to find somewhere to live. Meanwhile, _____ him all the love that he needs.
Jenny Torr
Brighton

2 I decided to give it all up and change my life dramatically three years ago. Since then, _____ the most exciting three years of my life. It can be scary, but if you don't do it, you won't know what you've missed. I don't think _____ . Go for it.
Mike Garfield
Manchester

3 He's using you. I think _____ . It's time for him to go. Twenty-four is too old to be living with his parents. He's got to take responsibility for himself. And _____ about his drug-taking. Sometimes you have to be cruel to be kind.
Tony Palmer
Harrow

4 Why _____ it? He isn't their slave, they don't own him. And I also can't stand the way people use their mobiles in restaurants, on trains and buses. They think that the people around them are invisible and can't hear. _____ .
Jane Sands
London

5 I think _____ before she gives up her job and goes to live abroad. Does she think that the sun will always shine? If there is something in her life that makes her unhappy now, this will follow her. She should take her time _____ .
Nigella Lawnes
Bristol

6 _____ ! He should have a word with his company and come to an arrangement with them. Why can't he turn it off sometimes? Mobile phones are great, and if he's got one for free, _____ . They are one of the best inventions ever.
Pete Hardcastle
Birmingham

3 Where do these lines go? Put a letter in the gaps.
a … you should tell him to leave home.
b … she should be very careful …
c … you should help him …
d … you should worry.
e He must keep it!
f … before making a decision.
g It is so rude.
h … he's very lucky.
i I have had…
j … you must tell the police …
k … you've got to give …
l … should he accept …

T 8.5 Listen and check.

4 Which letter writer … ?

- suggests waiting
- thinks love is the answer
- has been adventurous
- thinks that employers shouldn't exploit their employees
- loves mobile phones
- suggests being tough

The readers make very different suggestions. Who do you agree with?

What do you think?

- How old are children when they leave home in your country?
- What do you think of people who use mobile phones in public?
- Do you think older people should act their age? Why/Why not?
- 'You have to be cruel to be kind'. Can you think of an example?

Roleplay

With a partner, choose a situation and roleplay the conversation.

- Polly and one of her friends
- Jason and his boss
- Sarah and her husband

Group work

In groups, write a letter to a problem page.

Exchange your letters and write a reply. Try to express sympathy with the problem and give some explanation, as well as practical advice.

VOCABULARY
Words that go together

1 Many verbs and nouns go together.

tell a story   leave home

Look at the chart on the right. Match a verb with a complement. They all appear in the letters and problems on p66–67.

Look at the letters again and check your answers.

2 Close your books. Try to remember the sentences that include the phrases from the box.

3 Two nouns can go together. There are no rules about spelling.

post office   headache   horse-race

The stress is usually on the first word.

Match the nouns to make new words.

alarm	cream
car	glasses
traffic	table
credit	coat
ice	lights
sun	card
time	park
rain	clock

hair	case
sun	drier
ear	quake
sign	post
book	ring
rush	lighter
cigarette	set
earth	hour

T 8.6 Listen and check.

4 Choose a word and give a definition to the class. Can they guess the word?

You use it to pay for things.

A credit card.

That's right.

Verbs	Complements
live	being silly
write	your age
stop	abroad
act	responsibility
take	poetry
take	your job
stay	what you've missed
don't know	a word with someone
have to be	in bed
give up	your time
have	cruel to be kind

EVERYDAY ENGLISH

At the doctor's

1 Complete the chart with an illness or a symptom.

| diarrhoea |
| food poisoning |
| 'flu |

It hurts when I walk on it.
My glands are swollen, and it hurts when I swallow.
I can't stop sneezing and my nose is runny.

Illnesses	Symptoms
I've got a cold.	
I've got _____ .	I've got a temperature, my whole body aches, and I feel awful.
I've twisted my ankle.	
I've got _____ .	I keep going to the toilet.
I've got a sore throat.	
I've got _____ .	I keep being sick, and I've got diarrhoea.

What's the difference between these sentences?

I feel sick.   I was sick last night.

2 Put the sentences in the correct order.

- [1] I didn't feel very well.
- [ ] She took my temperature and examined me.
- [ ] After a few days, I started to feel better.
- [ ] I went to the surgery and saw the doctor.
- [ ] I went to the chemist's, paid for the prescription, and got some antibiotics.
- [ ] I phoned the doctor's surgery and made an appointment.
- [ ] She told me I had an infection.
- [ ] I explained what was wrong.
- [ ] She gave me a prescription.

3 **T 8.7** You will hear a conversation between Manuel, a student from Chile, and a doctor. Answer the questions.

1 What are Manuel's symptoms?
2 What questions does the doctor ask?
3 What does the doctor think is the matter with Manuel?
4 What does she prescribe?
5 What advice does she give him?
6 Does he have to pay for anything?

4 Look at the tapescript on p119. Practise with a partner.

5 Make similar conversations with other symptoms.

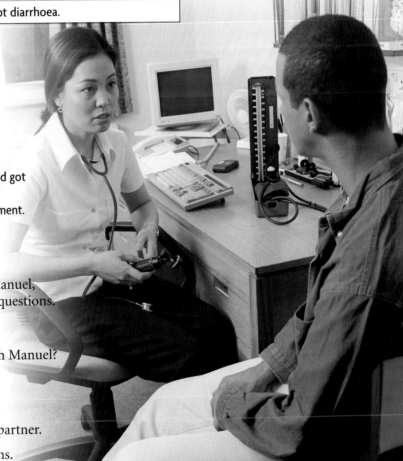

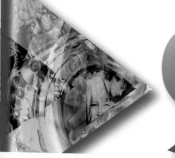

9 Going places

Time clauses · *if* · Hot verbs · In a hotel

STARTER

What do you think you will do if the weather is nice this weekend?
What will you do when you get home tonight?

THE GAP YEAR
Time and conditional clauses

1 Clare and her friend Ally are having a gap year. Complete
the sentences with phrases from the box below.

1 We're travelling round the world . . . **[c]**
2 We're going to leave . . . ☐
3 ☐ . . . we're going to learn to scuba dive on the
   Great Barrier Reef.
4 ☐ . . . we'll look after each other.
5 ☐ . . . we're going to the USA.
6 We can stay with my American cousins . . . ☐
7 Our parents will be worried . . . ☐
8 We'll stay in the States . . . ☐

---

a while we're in Los Angeles.
b If we get ill,
c before we go to university.
d until our visa runs out.
e When we're in Australia,
f as soon as we have enough money.
g if we don't keep in touch.
h After we leave Australia,

T 9.1 Listen and check.

2 Cover the box. Practise the sentences.

GRAMMAR SPOT

1 Underline the words in the box that introduce the clauses, e.g. *while*

2 Which tense are all the verbs in the box? Do they refer to the present or the future?

3 What are the different future forms in Clare and Ally's sentences?

4 What's the difference between these sentences? Which one is sure? Which one is possible?
   When I get home, I'll have something to eat.
   If there isn't any food, I'll get a pizza.

▶▶ **Grammar Reference 9.1–9.3 p125**

PRACTICE

when, as soon as

1 Complete the sentences with your ideas.

When I get home...

As soon as this lesson finishes...

If I win, ...

After I leave school...

While I'm in New York...

... before I get too old.

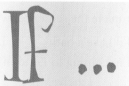

T 9.2 Listen and compare your answers.

What if . . . ?

2 Look at these hopes for the future. Make sentences using *If ... will ...*

If I don't go out so much, I'll do more work.
If I do more work, I'll ...

If ...

I don't go out so much
↓
do more work
↓
pass my exams
↓
go to university
↓
study medicine
↓
become a doctor
↓
earn a good salary.

If ...

I stop smoking
↓
have more money
↓
save some every week
↓
be rich when I'm thirty
↓
have my own business
↓
make a lot of money
↓
retire when I'm forty.

What will you do?

3 Work with a partner. One of you is going skiing for the first time. The other sees all the problems. Use these ideas to help you.

- don't like the food
- it rains
- don't learn to ski
- hurt yourself
- there's nothing to do in the evening
- don't make any friends
- lose your money
- get lost in a snowstorm

Make a similar conversation about going on safari for the first time.

Discussing grammar

4 Complete the sentences with *when, if, before,* or *until.*

1 I'll have a bath _____ I go to bed.
2 I'm coming to London tomorrow. I'll ring you _____ I arrive.
3 _____ it's a nice day tomorrow, we can go swimming.
4 Wait here _____ I get back.
5 _____ you have any problems, just ask for help.
6 I want to get home _____ it gets dark.
7 I'm going to have driving lessons _____ I pass my test.
8 Give me your address _____ you go home.

When I get to New York . . .

5 Put the verbs in brackets in the correct tense. Put *if, when, while,* or *as soon as* into each box.

Paul Bye, darling. Have a good trip to New York.
Mary Thanks. I 'll ring _____ (ring) you [as soon as] I arrive at the hotel.
Paul Fine. Remember I _____ (go) out with Henry tonight.
Mary Well, [ ] you _____ (be) out [ ] I _____ (ring), I _____ (leave) a message on the answerphone so you'll know I've arrived safely.
Paul Great. What time do you expect you'll be there?
Mary [ ] the plane _____ (arrive) on time, I _____ (be) at the hotel about 10.00.
Paul All right. Give me a ring [ ] you _____ (know) the time of your flight back, and I _____ (pick) you up at the airport.
Mary Thanks, darling. Don't forget to water the plants [ ] I _____ (be) away.
Paul Don't worry. I won't. Bye!

T 9.3 Listen and check.

LISTENING AND SPEAKING
Life in 2050

1 Read this description of the airline of the future:

> 'There will be just two crew members, a pilot and a dog. The pilot's job is to feed the dog. The dog's job is to bite the pilot if he tries to touch anything.'

What does this story say about life in the future?

2 You will hear an interview with Michio Kaku, Professor of Theoretical Physics at City University, New York. He has written a book, *Visions*, which explains how science will revolutionize the 21st century.

He is asked these questions.

- Are you optimistic about the future?
- Are we ready for the changes that will come?
- Is world population going to be a big problem?
- What will happen to people who don't have computers?
- Will there be a world government?
- Will we have control of everything?
- What are your reasons for pessimism?

Discuss your opinions on these subjects.

3 **T 9.4** Listen to the interview. Make notes on Michio Kaku's answers.

4 Answer the questions.

1 What does Michio Kaku say will continue into the twenty-first century?
2 How do some people react to the new technology? What is his reaction?
3 Why will the population of the world stop increasing?
4 Why will we need a world government?
5 What are some of the things we will be able to control?
6 What examples does he give of the behaviour of 'stupid' people?

What do you think?

Michio Kaku obviously believes in the power of science. What isn't he so sure about?
Do you agree?

READING AND SPEAKING
The world's first megalopolis

1 Are these statements about China true
or false?

- China is a communist country.
- One in five people in the whole world is Chinese.
- Chinese families can only have one child.
- Chinese people love tradition.
- Chinese people prefer bicycles to cars.
- The biggest city in the world is in China.

2 Read the newspaper article about Pearl River
City. Which of the subjects in exercise 1 are
talked about?

3 On the map find the following:

- Shenzhen
- Pearl River Estuary
- Guangzhou
- the Hopewell Highway

4 Answer the questions.

1 Has this city got a name yet?
2 Why is it ugly? Why is it exciting?
3 What are some of the statistics about
Shenzhen that make it a remarkable place?
4 In what ways is China changing? Why were
Deng Xiaoping's words significant?
5 How are the people changing?
Why do they want to own a car?
6 What does Shenzhen look like?
7 Why will this city be important in the 21st
century?
8 What do these numbers refer to?

1982	thousands
3 million	six months
less than ten years	two hours
40 million	four hours

What do you think?

- In groups, write what you think are the ten
largest cities in the world. Compare your list with
the class. Your teacher will tell you the answer.

- Make a list of some of the problems that these
cities face. Decide which are the three most
important problems. Compare your ideas with
the class.

**To the north of
Hong Kong, the
world's biggest city is
growing. It hasn't got
a new name yet, but
it will probably be
called Pearl River City.
Jonathon Glancey
visits this ugly,
exciting mess.**

Megalopolis

The town of Shenzhen, just forty kilometres north of Hong Kong, is the world's biggest building site. In 1982 it was a fishing village with two main roads, fields, and a population of 30,000. Now it has a population of 3 million. It is growing at an incredible speed. It is spreading north towards Guangzhou (also known as Canton) and west towards Macau. The Chinese government hopes that in less than ten years this area will be the biggest city on earth, with a population of 40 million people.

China is changing. It is no longer a country where absolutely everything is owned and controlled by the state. Developers are welcome. As Deng Xiaoping, the Chinese leader, said in 1992, 'To get rich is glorious'. The old China of bicycles and Little Red Books is disappearing. A world of mobile phones and capitalism is arriving.

The Chinese people seem to welcome dramatic change. They don't worry about losing traditional ways of life. They want the new. As the posters on the sides of the highways shout, 'Development is the only way.'

Shenzhen is a shocking place, like nowhere else on earth that I have ever seen. It is a city with no boundaries and no centre. There are new concrete office blocks, factories, and housing blocks as far as the eye can see. Not just dozens of new buildings, nor even hundreds, but thousands. And it is all happening so fast. It takes just six months to design, build, and finish a 60-storey, air-conditioned skyscraper. As one architect said to me, 'If you move too slowly here, someone will walk over you.'

The new Hopewell Highway runs from Shenzhen to Guangzhou, and it takes just two hours to do the 123 kilometres. This superhighway will become the main street of a huge new city, as it gets bigger and bigger until the east meets the west, and the countryside in the middle disappears under concrete.

There will of course be more and more cars on the road. People don't want bicycles. If you have a car, it means you have made money. So the traffic will be like in Bangkok, where people spend four hours commuting every day. People eat and work in their car.

Pearl River City very nearly exists. It will probably be the world's First City, the greatest city on earth. It won't be beautiful, but its power, energy, and wealth will be felt in all corners of the world.

VOCABULARY
Hot verbs – *take*, *get*, *do*, and *make*

1 The verbs *take*, *get*, *do*, and *make* are very common in English. Find these examples in the text about China:

> **get** rich   it **gets** bigger and bigger   you have **made** money
> it **takes** two hours **to do** 123 kilometres

2 Here are some more examples.
  A How long does it take you to get ready in the morning?
  B It takes me about fifteen minutes.
  A How long does it take you to get to school?
  B I can get here in twenty minutes.
  A Do you get tired in the evening?
  B Yes. Especially if I've done a lot of homework.
  A Do you make a lot of mistakes in English?
  B Well, I do my best, but I still make a few mistakes.
  Ask and answer the same questions with a partner.

3 Put the words and phrases from the box in the correct column.

> some shopping   back home   two tablets a day   a cold
> angry   sure   friends   up your mind   a photo
> somebody out for a meal   me a favour   a reservation
> on well with someone   a complaint   care

TAKE	GET	DO	MAKE

4 Complete the sentences with one of the verb phrases. Use the correct form of the verb.

1 I _____ while I was in town. I bought myself a new jumper.
2 'I don't know if I love Tom or Henry.' '_____ . You can't marry both of them.'
3 Bye-bye! See you soon. _____ of yourself.
4 Aachoo! Oh dear. I think _____ .
5 'Are the doors locked?' 'I think so, but I'll just _____ ?'

T 9.5 Listen and check.

5 Discuss these questions with a partner.
- How long does it take to get from your school to the station? From your home to work?
- When did you last do someone a favour/make a complaint/take a photo/get angry?
- What time did you get home last night?
- Do you get on with your parents/your neighbours?
- Do you find it easy to make friends?
- Is your English getting better?

EVERYDAY ENGLISH
In a hotel

1 What is the best hotel in your town? What facilities does the hotel have?

2 Ask and answer questions with a partner about the Grand Hotel.

> *Where's the conference centre?*

> *On the second floor.*

The Grand Hotel
♦♦♦

Ground Floor	Reception
	City Bar
First Floor	Dining Room
	Buckingham Rooms
Second Floor	Conference Centre
Top Floor	Panorama Restaurant
Basement	Gym
	Swimming pool

3 Put the lines from the telephone conversation between the receptionist and client in the right order.

Receptionist Hello, the Grand Hotel. Cathy speaking. How can I help you?

Client reservation / make / like / a / I'd / to / please

_____ .

Receptionist Certainly. When is it for?

Client It's for two nights, the thirteenth and the fourteenth of this month.

Receptionist single / want / do / room / or / double / a / And / you / a

_____ ?

Client A single, please.

Receptionist OK. Yes, that's fine. I have a room for you. And your name is?

Client Robert Palmer.

much / you / Can / it / tell / how / is / me

_____ ?

Receptionist Yes. That's £95 a night. Can I have a credit card number, please?

Client Yes, sure. It's a Visa. 4929 7983 0621 8849.

Receptionist Thank you.

number / could / And / phone / I / have / a

_____ ?

Client Uh huh. 01727 489962.

Receptionist That's fine.

forward / look / seeing / on / you / We / to / thirteenth / the

_____ . Bye-bye.

Client Thanks a lot. Goodbye.

T 9.6 Listen and check.

4 With a partner, roleplay the conversation between Robert Palmer and the receptionist as he checks into the hotel.

> *Good evening.*

> *Hello. I have a reservation. My name's Robert Palmer.*

5 Roleplay these conversations with your partner. Phone Reception from your room. Make these requests.

- You can't get the TV to work.
- You'd like an extra pillow.
- You'd like to order Room Service.
- You'd like a wake-up call at 7.00 tomorrow morning.

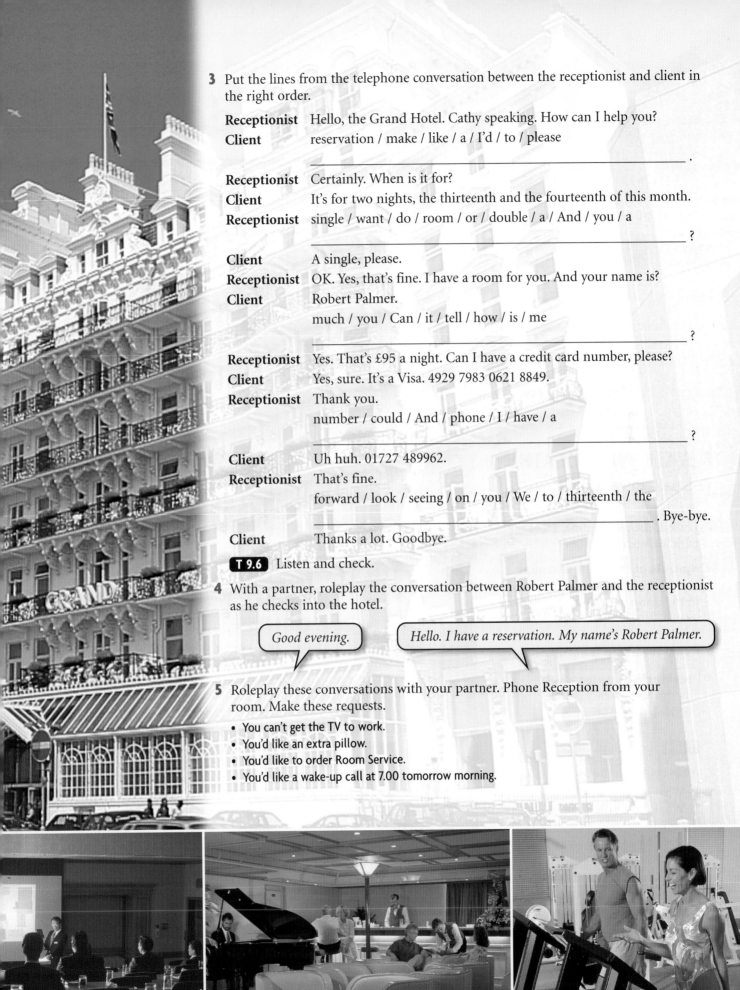

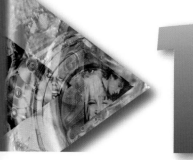

10 Scared to death

Verb patterns 2 - *manage to, used to* • *-ed/-ing* adjectives • Exclamations

STARTER

1 What are these people afraid of? How do they feel?

2 What are you afraid of? Why?

A WALK WITH DEATH
Verb patterns and infinitives

1 Look at the photograph. Does the path look safe to you?

Read about Paul Lay's adventure. How did he feel at different times in the story?

2 Complete the text using these words.

> began to feel   started aching
> used to have   went camping
> decided to stand up

T 10.1 Listen and check.

3 Answer the questions.

1 What is Paul Lay's hobby?
2 What did he use to do with his father?
3 Does he go to the same place every year?
4 Is the King's Way in good condition?
5 Why couldn't he have a rest?
6 Why didn't he enjoy the walk?

Don t look down

Paul Lay dances with death in the mountains of southern Spain

I have always enjoyed walking. When I was a boy, I used to go walking at weekends with my father. We (1) _____ and climbing together.

I try to visit a new place every year. Last year I decided to walk a path in Spain called *El Camino del Rey*, which means the King's Way. It is one of the highest and most dangerous footpaths in Europe. It used to be very safe, but now it is falling down.

I took a train to the village of El Chorro and started to walk towards the mountains. I was very excited. Then the adventure began.

The path was about three feet wide and there were holes in it. It (2) _____ a handrail, but not any more. I didn't know what to do – should I go on my hands and knees, or stand up? I (3) _____ and walk very slowly. At times the path was only as wide as my two boots. I stopped to have a rest, but there was nowhere to sit.

I (4) _____ very frightened. It was impossible to look down or look up. I was concentrating so hard that my body (5) _____ . There was no thrill of danger, no enjoyment of the view. I thought I was going to die.

I finally managed to get to the end. I was shaking, and I was covered in sweat from heat and fear. I fell to the ground, exhausted.

GRAMMAR SPOT

1 Are these verbs followed by the infinitive or *-ing* in the text?

enjoy try decide start begin manage

2 Find the examples of *used to* + infinitive. *Used to* expresses a past action which doesn't happen any more.

*I **used to** play games with my brother, but now I don't.*

Notice the pronunciation /juːst tʊ/.

3 Complete these examples from the text.

I used to go _____ at weekends.

I didn't know what _____ .

I stopped _____ a rest.

It was impossible _____ down.

There was nowhere _____ .

▶▶ **Grammar Reference 10.1–10.4 p126**

PRACTICE

Discussing grammar

1 Complete these sentences with the verb *ski* in the correct form.

1 I go _____ every winter.
2 I started _____ when I was six.
3 I tried _____ down the mountain, but it was too steep.
4 My instructor made me _____ down the steep mountain.
5 I enjoy _____ very much.
6 Dave used _____ when he was younger, but not any more.

2 Choose the correct form.

1 I've decided *stop / to stop / stopping* smoking.
2 I managed *find / to find / finding* my passport.
3 Let's go *shop / to shop / shopping*!
4 Please let me *go / to go / going* to the party!
5 Would you like something *eat / to eat / eating*?
6 I need a recipe for a cake that's easy *make / to make / making*.

When I was young, I used to ...

3 **T 10.2** Listen to James talking about his childhood and his life now. Complete the chart. Write one sentence with *used to* for each question.

	Life as a child
1 What/do at the weekend?	
2 What/do in the evening?	
3 Where/go on holiday?	
4 What sports/play?	
5 What TV programmes/like?	
6 What food/like?	

James

Ask and answer the questions above with a partner about your life now and your life as a child.

> *What do you do at the weekend?*

> *I usually go shopping and …*

> *What did you do when you were a child?*

> *I used to play with my friends and …*

Infinitives

4 Why do you go to these places?

> *Why do you go to the hairdresser's?*

> *To have a haircut.*

- the post office
- a petrol station
- a bookshop
- the newsagent's
- the library
- the market

With your partner, ask and answer questions about more places.

5 Make sentences with a line in **A**, a word in **B**, and an infinitive in **C**.

A	B	C
1 I'm hungry. I need	how	to say to you.
2 I'm going to a posh party, but I don't know	anything	to talk to.
3 My CD player's broken. Can you show me	where	to eat.
4 Don't talk to me. I have	somebody	to wear.
5 Do I turn left or right? I don't know	how much	to repair it?
6 I'm bored. I haven't got	nothing	to do.
7 'Can you get some meat?' 'Sure. Tell me	something	to go.
8 I feel lonely. I need	what	to buy.'

T 10.3 Think of some replies. Then listen and compare your answers.

Check it

6 Choose the correct form.

1 I went to the shops *for to buy / for buy / to buy* some shoes.
2 Do you enjoy *dance / dancing / to dance*?
3 When I was young, I used *to go / go / going* ice-skating.
4 He told me he loves me. I didn't know what *say / to say / saying*.
5 When we were on holiday, we went *swim / to swim / swimming* every day.

VOCABULARY
-ed/-ing adjectives

1 How can you describe the experiences below? Use an adjective from the box.

> frightening exciting surprising terrifying boring exhausting

1 You get stuck in a lift.
2 You go on a 15-mile walk, then climb three mountains.
3 You go on the biggest roller coaster in the world.
4 You find a spider in the bath.
5 Someone shows you their holiday photos for hours and hours …
6 Your teacher says 'You're all such wonderful students that I won't give you any more homework.'

2 How do the people in the photos feel?

He's frightened.

T 10.4 Listen and practise the pronunciation of these words.

> ! 1 *-ing* adjectives describe a situation, person, or thing.
>   an **interesting** life
>   a **boring** teacher
>   an **exciting** film
>
>   2 *-ed* adjectives describe how people feel.
>   I'm very **interested** in modern art.
>   We were **bored** at the end of the lesson.
>   She's **excited** about going on holiday tomorrow.

3 Complete the sentences. Use one of these adjectives.

excit- frighten- bor- interest- confus- disappoint- worry/worri- surpris-	-ed -ing

1 'I met a famous film star today.' 'Really? How _____ !'
2 'I spent four hours going round a museum.' 'Was it _____ ?'
   'No, it was _____ .'
3 'I haven't heard from my parents for two months.' 'You must be _____ .'
4 'Wow, Maria! What are you doing here?' 'Why are you so _____ to see me?'
5 I failed my exam. I worked really hard for it. I'm so _____ .
6 'A man started to follow me home last night.' 'Weren't you _____ ?'
7 My computer's broken, and I don't understand the manual. It's so _____ .

T 10.5 Close your books. Listen to the beginnings of the lines. Complete them.

4 What have you seen on television or in the cinema recently? What books have you read? What did you think of them? Tell a partner.

> I read a spy novel. It was very exciting.

> I saw a horror film. I thought it was frightening.

READING AND SPEAKING
Into the wild

1 Describe what you can see in the photograph. Which country do you think it is? What makes life difficult for people who live here?

2 Read the introductory paragraph and the words in **bold**. In pairs, decide whether these statements are true (✔) or false (✗).

- Chris McCandless died very young.
- He was killed by hunters.
- He didn't enjoy his life.
- He loved nature and a simple life.
- He wanted to die.
- He knew he was dying.

What do you want to know about Chris?

3 Read to the line ending "… *Thank you!' his diary reads.*" and answer the questions.

1 Did Chris keep in touch with his parents? When did they last hear from him?
2 Why did he get rid of his car and burn his money?
3 What did he need? What didn't he need?
4 In what way was his life rich?

4 Read to the line ending "… *I didn't know where he was.*" Choose the best answer.

1 Chris didn't get on with his father because his father
   - ☐ had a lot of money.
   - ☐ didn't let Chris work in the family business.
   - ☐ tried to tell Chris what to do.

2 When the parents didn't hear from Chris,
   - ☐ the police got in touch with them.
   - ☐ they got in touch with the police.
   - ☐ they did nothing.

3 In July 1992
   - ☐ his mother dreamt that she heard Chris calling her.
   - ☐ his mother is sure that she heard Chris calling her.
   - ☐ Chris phoned his mother for help.

5 Read to the end. Correct the mistakes in this summary.

> Chris got the train to Alaska, and arrived in May, 1992. He lived in a bus, and there was a bed and a bath in it. He was very happy. There was lots to eat – small animals, and fruit and vegetables, which he grew himself.
>
> After five months of living alone, he started to feel ill. He had no strength because he was eating poisonous plants, but he didn't know that this was the reason. He continued eating. He died of food poisoning.
>
> He knew he was dying. He wrote a letter to his parents, and took a photo of himself. He seemed happy to die in these circumstances.

What do you think?

- What was important to Chris? What wasn't important?
- What do you think he was trying to do?
- Why do young people feel the need to break away from their parents?

In April 1992, Chris McCandless, a young man from a wealthy American family, hitchhiked to Alaska. Four months later, his dead body was found by a group of hunters. Jon Krakauer investigated the story.

When Chris McCandless graduated from Emory University, Atlanta, in June 1990, he sent his parents a letter containing his final reports. His letter ended 'Say 'Hi' to everyone for me.'

No one in Chris's family ever heard from him again.

He drove west out of Atlanta, and invented a new life for himself with a new name. He left his car in some woods and burned all his money, because, as he wrote in his diary, **'I need no possessions. I can survive with just nature.'**

For the next two years, he hitched to various parts of the United States and

Into the wild

Mexico. He wanted the freedom to go where he wanted and to work when he needed. For him, his life was very rich. '**God, it's great to be alive. Thank you! Thank you!**' his diary reads.

Chris came from a comfortable background. His father had a business which he ran efficiently, and he controlled his own family in a similar way. Chris and his father didn't get on. When his parents didn't hear from him for several months, they contacted the police, but they could do nothing. In July 1992, two years after Chris left Atlanta, his mother woke in the middle of the night. 'I could hear Chris calling me. I wasn't dreaming. He was begging, 'Mom! Help me!' But I couldn't help him because I didn't know where he was.'

Chris's dream was to spend some time in Alaska, and this is where he went in April 1992. In early May, after a few days in the Alaskan bush, Chris found an old bus which hunters used for shelter. It had a bed and a stove. He decided to stay there for a while. '**Total freedom,**' he wrote. '**My home is the road.**'

> I need no possessions. I can survive with just nature.

However, reality soon changed the dream. He was hungry, and it was difficult to find enough to eat. He shot ducks, squirrels, birds, and sometimes a moose, and with these he ate wild potatoes, wild mushrooms, and berries. He was losing a lot of weight.

On July 30 he wrote, '**Extremely weak. Fault of potato seed. Can't stand up. Starving. Danger.**' It seems that Chris was eating a part of the wild potato plant that was poisonous. He couldn't get out of the bus to look for food. '**I am trapped in the wild,**' he wrote on August 5.

He became weaker and weaker as he was starving to death. His final note says, '**I have had a good life and thank the Lord. Goodbye and may God bless all!**'

Then he crawled into his sleeping bag and lost consciousness. He probably died on August 18. One of the last things he did was to take a photo of himself, one hand holding his final note, the other hand raised in a brave goodbye. His face is horribly thin, but he is smiling in the picture, and the look in his eyes says 'I am at peace.'

LISTENING AND SPEAKING
It was just a joke

1 In Britain, your eighteenth birthday is important, because it is the birthday when you become an adult. Which birthdays are special in your country? What do people do?

2 You will hear a boy called Jamie describing what he did on his friend's eighteenth birthday. It was just a joke, but it looked serious! Look at the pictures. What do you think happened? Check that you know these words.

to kidnap · a balaclava · to tie up · a blindfold · a witness

3 **T 10.6** Listen to Jamie being interviewed. Does he tell the story in the same order as the pictures?

4 Answer the questions.

1 Identify these people in the pictures.

> Tom   Jamie   Dave   Andrew
> the witness

2 Imagine who says these lines in the story.

- I've had a really good idea for Tom's birthday!
- Lie on the ground! Don't move!
- Please let me go!
- Send the police immediately!
- Come and help. This looks really serious.
- Happy birthday, dear Tom!
- You *****s! I thought you were my friends!
- I knew it was you from the beginning!
- Excuse me, gentlemen. Can I just ask you a few questions?
- I think we have a bit of a confession to make.

Roleplay

With a partner, roleplay one of these conversations and retell the story.

- Tom talking to his girlfriend
- the witness talking to the emergency services
- Jamie talking to the policeman

EVERYDAY ENGLISH
Exclamations with *so* and *such*

1 **T 10.7** Read and listen to the sentences.

Tom was scared.   He was very scared.   He was so scared!

Do you think this use of *so* is more written or spoken? What effect does it have?

2 Look at the sentences. When do we use *so*, *such a(n)*, *such*, *so many*, and *so much*?

> We were all *so worried*!
> Mike's *such an idiot*!
> It was *such a good idea* of Jamie's!
> He has *such crazy friends*!
> We had *such awful weather* on holiday!
> There are *so many places* I want to go to!
> I've got *so much work*!

3 Complete the sentences in **A** with *so*, *such a*, *such*, *so many*, or *so much*. Then match them with the sentences in **B**.

A	B
1 Their house is _____ mess!	I could eat a horse.
2 There were _____ people at the party!	I don't know where it's all gone.
3 I'm _____ hungry!	You really didn't have to.
4 Jane and Pete are _____ nice people!	She understands every word I say.
5 I've spent _____ money this week!	There was nowhere to dance.
6 A present! For me? You're _____ kind!	Thank you so much for inviting us.
7 We've had _____ nice time!	But I can't stand their kids.
8 Molly's _____ clever dog!	I don't know how they live in it.

T 10.8 Listen and check. Practise the exclamations.

4 What can you say … ?

- at the end of a long journey

- when you finish an interesting book with a sad ending
- as you go round a friend's new flat
- at the end of a wonderful meal
- in a row with your boyfriend/girlfriend
- at the end of a great English lesson

11 Things that changed the world

Passives · Verbs and nouns that go together · Notices

STARTER

1 Make true sentences from the chart.
2 What is made and grown in your country?

Champagne Whisky Rice Rolls Royce cars Nikon cameras Coffee Pineapples	is are	made in grown in	Japan. France. England. Hawaii. Brazil. China. Scotland.

SOLD WORLDWIDE
Passives

1 Do you drink Coca-Cola? Do you think these facts about Coca-Cola are true (✓) or false (✗)?

1 ☐ 1.6 billion gallons are sold every day.
2 ☐ Coca-Cola is drunk in every country in the world.
3 ☐ It was invented in the USA.
4 ☐ It is nearly 100 years old.

Read the story of Coca-Cola and check your ideas.

Things go better with
Coca-Cola

Coca-Cola is enjoyed all over the world.

1.6 billion gallons are sold every year, in over one hundred and sixty countries. The drink was invented by Dr John Pemberton in Atlanta as a health drink on 8 May 1886, but it was given the name Coca-Cola by his partner, Frank Robinson, because it was originally made from the coca plant. In the first year, only nine drinks a day were sold.

The business was bought by a man called Asa Candler in 1888, and the first factory was opened in Dallas, Texas, in 1895. Coca-Cola is still made there. Billions of bottles and cans have been produced since 1895, but the recipe is still kept secret!

Diet Coke has been made since 1982, and over the years many clever advertisements have been used to sell the product. It is certain that Coca-Cola will be drunk far into the twenty-first century.

Coca-Cola goes along...for *the pause that refreshes*

GRAMMAR SPOT

GRAMMAR SPOT

1 Nearly all the verb forms in the text about Coca-Cola are in the passive. The passive is formed with the verb *to be* and the past participle.

   Champagne **is made** in France.
   Pineapples **are grown** in Hawaii.

2 Read the text again and write the passive verb forms under these headings.

Present Simple	**Past Simple**	**Present Perfect**	*will* **Future**
is enjoyed	was invented	have been produced	

3 What is the main interest of the text? Dr John Pemberton? Frank Robinson? Coca-Cola?

   When we are more interested in the object of the active sentence, we use the passive.
   Active: Dr John Pemberton invented Cola-Cola.
   Passive: Cola-Cola was invented by Dr John Pemberton.

▶▶ **Grammar Reference 11.1 p127**

2 Don't look at the text! Look at the passive verb forms in the columns above and try to remember the whole sentence.

Coca-Cola is enjoyed all over ...

It was invented by ...

PRACTICE

Active and passive

1 Complete these sentences.

Active	Passive
1 They make Rolls Royce cars in England.	Rolls Royce cars _are made_ in England.
2 They _____ rice in China.	Rice is grown in China.
3 Bell invented the telephone in 1876.	The telephone _____ by Bell in 1876.
4 Thieves _____ two pictures from the museum last night.	Two pictures were stolen from the museum last night.
5 They have built three new factories this year.	Three new factories _____ this year.
6 They _____ the picture for £3,000.	The picture has been sold for £3,000.
7 The factory will produce 10,000 cars next year.	10,000 cars _____ next year.
8 _____ they _____ many cars last year?	Were many cars made last year?
9 Bell didn't invent the television.	The television _____ by Bell.

2 Put the verbs in brackets in the correct tense, active or passive.

The History of the Hamburger

The hamburger is the most eaten food in the whole world. The first hamburgers (1) _____ (make) and sold in Connecticut in 1895 by an American chef called Louis Lassen. Louis (2) _____ (call) them hamburgers because he (3) _____ (give) the recipe by sailors from Hamburg in Germany. Hamburgers (4) _____ (become) a favourite in America in the early part of the twentieth century. Their popularity (5) _____ (grow) even more after the Second World War, when they (6) _____ (buy) in large quantities by teenagers who (7) _____ (prefer) fast food to family meals. In 1948 two brothers, Dick and Mac McDonald (8) _____ (open) a drive-in hamburger restaurant in San Bernardino, California. Since then over 25,000 McDonald's restaurants (9) _____ (open) worldwide and now 35 million McDonald's hamburgers (10) _____ (eat) every day in 115 countries from India to the Arctic Circle.

Questions and answers

3 Match the question words and answers.

When?	Louis Lassen.
Where?	In Connecticut.
Who?	In 1895.
Why?	In 1948.
How many?	Because the recipe came from Hamburg.
	25,000.
	35 million.

4 Complete the questions using the passive. Ask and answer them with a partner.

When was the first hamburger made?

In 1895.

T 11.1 Listen and check.

5 Complete the conversations and practise them with a partner.

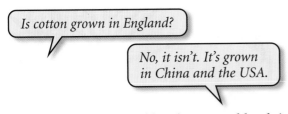

Is cotton grown in England?

No, it isn't. It's grown in China and the USA.

1 **A** Are Coca-Cola and hamburgers sold *only* in America?
   B No, they aren't. They _____ .
2 **A** Was Cola-Cola invented by Louis Lassen?
   B No, it _____ .
3 **A** Were the first hamburgers made in 1948?
   B No, they _____ .
4 **A** Was the first McDonald's restaurant opened in New York?
   B No, it _____ .
5 **A** Have 2,500 restaurants now been opened worldwide?
   B No, not 2,500. _____ .

T 11.2 Listen and check.

Check it

6 Underline the correct word or words in each sentence.
1 Where *was / were* these shoes made?
2 I was given this watch *by / from* my aunt.
3 Someone *has stolen / has been stolen* my bag!
4 The newsagent *sells / is sold* stamps.
5 British policemen *don't carry / aren't carried* guns.
6 All the beer was *drank / drunk* by nine o'clock.
7 Have all the sandwiches *eaten / been eaten*?

VOCABULARY
Verbs and nouns that go together

1 In each box below, one noun does *not* go with the verb. Which one?

2 Work with a partner. Choose two nouns from each box, and write two sentences using the verb. Read your sentences to the class.

Rice is grown in China.
The ship carried a cargo of tobacco and cotton.

3 Which six nouns do not go with the verbs? Which verbs do they go with? Complete the sentences with the correct verbs.

1 _____ hello to your parents from me when you see them.
2 I was late for work because I _____ the bus.
3 This is my grandfather's watch. He _____ it every day until he died.
4 I _____ just _____ a good idea. Let's eat out tonight.
5 My uncle _____ £500 on the stock exchange.
6 We _____ a complaint to the manager because our meal was so bad.

READING AND SPEAKING
Three plants that changed the world

1 Read the introduction to a book review. What is the book about?

Seeds of Change

By Henry Hobhouse
Reviewed by Donald Crisp

History books are full of the ways in which the actions of men and women have changed the world, but what about plants? Which plants have changed history? Henry Hobhouse, farmer and journalist, discusses this topic in his fascinating and illuminating book *Seeds of Change*.

2 Look at these drawings. Do you recognize the three plants?

3 All the words below appear in the article about the plants. Which words do you think go with which plant? Some go with more than one.

nouns:	addict soil fabric silk plantation slaves lung cancer luxury
verbs:	chain-smoke inhale ban sweeten refine chew harvest

4 Work in three groups.
Group A Read about tobacco.   **Group B** Read about sugar.   **Group C** Read about cotton.

5 Which words from exercise 3 are in your text? What are the bad effects of the plant? What are the good effects? Discuss in your group.

6 Compare plants with two students from the other groups. Answer the questions.

Which plant (or plants) . . .
- has been grown for thousands of years?
- was known as white gold? Why?
- was once thought to be a luxury?
- caused the American Civil War? Why?
- was the main American export until 1820?
- became the main American export after 1820?
- was harvested by slaves?
- has caused the death of many people?

What do you think?

- Which of the three plants has *most* changed history? How?
- Which plant has done the greatest good? Which has done the greatest harm?

Tobacco

For thousands of years **tobacco** was used by the American Indians with no ill-effect. In the 16th century it was brought to Europe. This early tobacco was mixed with soil and rather dirty. It was chewed or smoked in pipes only by men – women thought it smelly and disgusting.

It was first grown commercially in America in the 17th century on slave plantations. In the 18th century new technology refined tobacco and the first cigarettes were produced. By the 1880s huge factories were producing cigarettes which were clean and easy to smoke. Chain-smoking and inhaling became possible and by the middle of the 20th century tobacco addicts, both men and women, were dying of lung cancer in great numbers.

Nowadays cigarette smoking is banned in many places, especially in the USA. But until 1820 tobacco was America's main export, and still today their tobacco industry makes over $4.2 billion a year.

Sugar

Sugar cane was grown in India thousands of years ago. In Roman times it was known in Europe as a great luxury, and it was rare and expensive for many centuries after that. In 1493 Columbus took a sugar plant with him to the West Indies, where it grew so well that huge plantations were started by Europeans and worked on by slaves. The slaves were shipped across the Atlantic from Africa, packed sometimes one on top of the other in chains, on a journey that took six weeks. Many died. The empty ships then carried the sugar back to Europe. So much money was made that sugar was known as 'white gold'.

Sugar is used to sweeten food and make sweets and chocolate. It is addictive but unnecessary. By the 16th century the English were the greatest sugar-eaters in history. Elizabeth I lost *all* her teeth because she ate so much of it.

Cotton

Cotton has been grown for over five thousand years in places as far apart as Mexico, China, Egypt, and India. It was first planted in America in 1607. Before 1800 cotton was a great luxury, more expensive than silk, because so many workers were needed to pick it. However, a huge increase in the number of slaves in the American South resulted in much greater cotton production and a fall in the price. This, and the new technology of the industrial revolution, made cotton the cheapest fabric in history. By 1820 cotton was making more money for the USA than tobacco, and more money worldwide than sugar.

The American Civil War of 1861–1865 was fought because the Southern States wanted to form a separate country, so that they could continue to keep slaves on their cotton plantations. Slavery was banned in the Northern States in 1808. 500,000 soldiers were killed in the war.

LISTENING AND SPEAKING
The world's most common habit: chewing gum

1 Do you chew gum? How often? Stand up and ask the students in the class. Complete the chart below.

NUMBER OF STUDENTS WHO CHEW GUM
... often _____
... sometimes _____
... rarely _____
... never _____

2 Discuss these questions as a class.

1 Who often chews gum? Who never chews gum?
2 When and where do you chew gum?
3 Where do you put it when it has lost its flavour?

3 You are going to listen to a radio programme about chewing gum. Check the meaning of these words. Which have an obvious connection with the topic of chewing gum? How?

skeleton *(n)*	to freshen (the breath) *(v)*	tree sap *(n)*
honey *(n)*	to wrap *(v)*	packet *(n)*
to hire *(v)*	billboard *(n) (Am. Eng.)*	

4 Read the statements below. Do you think they are true (✓) or false (✗)? Discuss with a partner.

1 ☐ One million tons of gum is chewed every year.
2 ☐ Chewing gum was invented in Sweden.
3 ☐ Chewing gum was found in the mouth of a nine thousand-year-old skeleton.
4 ☐ The first gum was made of tree sap and sugar.
5 ☐ Babies are born wanting to chew gum.
6 ☐ The ancient Greeks believed chewing gum was good for your health.
7 ☐ South American Indians made the first packets of chewing gum.
8 ☐ Chewing gum was taken to North America by the English.

T 11.3 Listen to part one of the programme and check your ideas. Correct the false sentences.

5 **T 11.4** Listen to part two of the programme. Answer the questions.

1 Who was William Wrigley?
2 What did he do to advertise chewing gum?
3 When did chewing gum become popular outside the USA?
4 What did the children shout?
5 What is today's chewing gum made of?

What do you think?

• Is chewing gum a common habit in your country?

• Is it considered a bad habit? Why/Why not?

• Is chewing gum good for you? Why/Why not?

EVERYDAY ENGLISH
Notices

1 When you first go to a foreign country, it can be difficult to understand notices. Here are some typical English notices. Match them with these places.

1 ☐ℓ a bank or a post office
2 ☐ a petrol station
3 ☐ a broken drinks machine
4 ☐ a road in a town
5 ☐ an airport
6 ☐ a pub
7 ☐ the Underground
8 ☐ a park
9 ☐ a zoo
10 ☐ a hotel
11 ☐ a railway station
12 ☐ a public toilet
13 ☐ a motorway

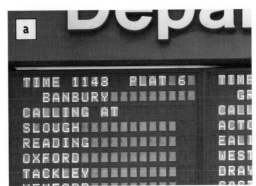

2 **T 11.5** Listen to five conversations. Where are the people?

3 Work with a partner. Choose two other places, and write conversations that could happen there. Read them to the class, and see if they can guess the place.

12 Dreams and reality

Second conditional · *might* · Phrasal verbs · Social expressions 2

STARTER

1 Which famous person would you like to meet? What would you talk about?

2 Which country would you like to visit? What would you do there?

3 If you won a lot of money, what would you buy? How much would you give to friends?

SWEET DREAMS
Second conditional

1 Read about Nicola. Which text describes her life? Which describes her dreams?

> I live in a flat with my Mum and my little brother. My Mum works in a hospital, so my Gran often looks after us and she helps my Mum. We have a budgie. I go to St Barnabas School and I wear a green uniform. I can only have sweets on Saturdays.

Nicola, aged 7

> If I were a princess, I'd live in a _____ . I'd have _____ to look after me. My Mum would be Queen, and she wouldn't work. I wouldn't go to school. I'd have a private _____ . I'd ride a white _____ , and I'd wear a long _____ . I could have all the _____ I wanted.

2 Complete the text on the right with these words.

| horse sweets palace dress teacher servants |

T 12.1 Listen and check. Then listen and repeat.

GRAMMAR SPOT

1   What tense describes Nicola's real life?
2   *If I lived in a palace, . . .*
    Does she live in a palace? What tense is *lived*?
        . . . I'd have servants.   (I'd = I would)
    Is this a dream or reality?
3   Complete the rule.
    We make unreal conditional clauses with *if* + the _____ tense.
    In the result clause, we use the auxiliary verb _____ + the infinitive.
4   Notice that *was* can change to *were* in the condition clause.
        If I were a princess, . . .

▶▶ **Grammar Reference 12.1 p128**

3 Look at the questions and short answers.

> *Where would she live?*

> *In a palace.*

> *Would her grandmother look after her?*

> *No, she wouldn't. She'd have servants.*

Ask and answer questions about Nicola's dreams with a partner.

- What . . . her mother do?
- . . . work?
- . . . Nicola go to school?
- What pet . . . have?
- What . . . wear?
- . . . have a lot of sweets?

PRACTICE

Discussing grammar

1 Make sentences from the chart.

	found	cakes and ice-cream,		feel better.
	were	the answer,		get a job in the police.
	knew	a car,		lose weight.
If I	had	taller,	I'd	buy a big house.
	didn't eat	so much,	I wouldn't	build more hospitals.
	didn't smoke	a lot of money,		keep it.
		president,		tell you.
		some money in the street,		give you a lift.

2 Put the verbs in the correct form.

1   If I _____ (be) rich, I _____ (travel) round the world. First I _____ (go) to Canada, then I _____ (go) to New York.
2   If he _____ (work) harder, he _____ (have) more money.
3   I _____ (go) to work if I _____ (feel) better, but I feel terrible.
4   If I _____ (can) speak perfect English, I _____ (not be) in this classroom.
5   'What _____ you _____ (do) if a stranger _____ (give) you £1 million?'

What would you do?

3 Discuss what you would do if …

- you came home and found a burglar.
- someone gave you a present that you really didn't like.
- you saw someone shoplifting.
- you found a wallet with a lot of money in it.
- you saw two people fighting in the street.

If I were you . . .

4 **T 12.2** We can give advice using *If I were you, I'd …*

> *I feel terrible! My head hurts, and I feel dizzy.*

> *If I were you, I'd go to bed.*

Work with a partner. Give the people advice about their problems.

1 I have no money.
2 My hair's awful.
3 I've got toothache.
4 I've had a row with my boyfriend.
5 My car won't start in the morning.
6 My neighbours make a lot of noise.

T 12.3 Listen and compare your answers.

WHO KNOWS?
might

1 **T 12.4** Listen to two students saying what they're going to do when they leave university. Complete the texts.

Ruth

> I _____ a holiday in Italy for a couple of weeks, staying in a villa in Tuscany. Then I _____ for a job. I _____ in the media – advertising or the BBC would be perfect.
> My sister and I _____ a flat together, somewhere central, so we _____ to start looking soon. I'm very excited about the future. And I'm also highly ambitious!

2 What are some of the certainties in Ruth's life?
She's having a holiday in Italy.

- . . . villa in Tuscany.
- . . . for a job.
- . . . flat together.
- . . . start looking soon.

3 What are some of the possibilities in Henry's life?
He might go to America.

- . . . restaurant for a bit.
- . . . Paris for a while.
- . . . French girl . . .

Henry

I'm not sure yet. Some friends have invited me to go to Long Island with them, so I might go to America. I'll have to earn some money, so I _____ in a restaurant for a bit.

I don't know what I want to do. I love France, so I _____ in Paris for a while. I could earn some money painting portraits in Montmartre. Who knows? I _____ a beautiful French girl and fall in love! Wouldn't that be wonderful!

GRAMMAR SPOT

1 *Might* means the same as *perhaps . . . will . . . .*
   What are you doing tonight?
   I don't know. I might go out, or I might stay at home.

2 *Might* is a modal auxiliary.
   Ann might come round tonight.
   I might not pass my exams.
   Do we add -*s* with *he/she/it*?
   Do we use *do/does* in the negative?

▶▶ **Grammar Reference 12.2 p128**

PRACTICE

Discussing grammar

1 Choose the correct verb in these sentences.

   1 'What's for supper?' '*We're having / we might have* lamb. It's in the oven.'
   2 'What time are we eating?' 'Don't worry. *It'll be / it might be* ready before your TV programme.'
   3 'Who's eating with us?' 'I've invited Jerry, but *he'll be / he might be* late. It depends on the traffic.'
   4 I'm going into town tomorrow. *I'm having / I might have* lunch with Jo at 1.00.
   5 'Are you going to have a winter holiday this year?' '*I am / I might*. I haven't decided yet.'

Possibilities

2 Make conversations with a partner about these future possibilities. One of you isn't sure about anything.

> *What are you doing tonight?*

> *I'm not sure. I might go out or I might stay at home.*

   1 What sort/car/buy?
     Fiat/Toyota
   2 Where/on holiday?
     Scotland/Spain
   3 What/have to eat?
     steak/fish
   4 Who/going to the dance with?
     ask Tony/ask Richard

3 Ask and answer questions with a partner about your possible future plans:

   • after the lesson   • at the weekend
   • this evening   • for your next holiday

Check it

4 Correct the mistakes in these sentences.

   1 If I'd have a car, I'd give you a lift.
   2 They'll call their baby Lily, but they aren't sure yet.
   3 I'd visit you more often if you wouldn't live so far away.
   4 I'm playing tennis tomorrow. I'm not sure.
   5 If I'm younger, I'll learn to play the piano, but I'm too old now.

READING AND LISTENING
Ghost stories

1 Do you believe in ghosts? What would you do if you saw a ghost? Would you talk to it? Would you run away?

2 You are going to read about a man called Aelwyn Roberts. He's a ghostbuster.

Do you think he . . . ?
- believes or doesn't believe in ghosts.
- tries to find ghosts.
- tries to get rid of ghosts.

Read the text and find out.

3 Are the statements true (✓) or false (✗)? Correct the false ones.
1 Mr Roberts is a social worker.
2 He helps to sort out problems for both people and ghosts.
3 He is sure that ghosts exist.
4 The boy knew it was his great-grandfather at the end of his bed.
5 The old man made the boy laugh.
6 Mr Roberts solved the boy's problem easily.
7 Ghosts are not usually members of the family.
8 Mr Roberts says you should never talk firmly to ghosts.

4 **T 12.5** Look at the newspaper extract on the right, then listen to an interview with Alice Lester.

Check that you know these words.

| brain scan   consultant   tumour   operation |

5 Answer the questions.
1 Did Alice Lester know she was ill before she heard the voices?
2 What was she doing when she first heard the voices?
3 What did the first voice tell her?
4 What happened while she was away on holiday?
5 What happened when she returned to London?
6 Did the consultant believe what she told him?
7 What did the voices finally tell her? How is she now?

What do you think?

- Do you think Alice Lester's story is a ghost story?

- Do you believe that Mr Roberts really gets rid of ghosts?

Telling stories

Do you know any ghost stories? In small groups, tell your ghost stories. Which is the most frightening?

Woman heard 'voices' telling her of tumour
by John Crutchley

The mysterious case of Alice Lester appeared in the British Medical Journal. Alice claims that she heard voices in her head which correctly told her that she had a brain tumour.

I'M A **GHOST**BUSTER, SAYS VICAR

Aelwyn Roberts, 79, used to be a vicar. He's retired now, but he still works as a ghostbuster. He helps people who have ghosts in their houses to get rid of them.

'I'm a kind of social worker for ghosts,' he explains. 'Some people die and they still have problems when they leave this world, so they come back again as ghosts to sort them out. I don't think ghosts *might* exist. I know they *do* exist.'

He says he has met thousands of ghosts trapped between this world and the next. He helps them sort out their problems so they can move on to the next world.

One example is typical. At exactly nine every night a three-year-old boy got out of bed and came downstairs. When his parents asked him to explain why, he said that

he saw an old man in a funny hat sitting on the end of the bed and the man told him to get out of his bed and go downstairs.

For Mr Roberts this was simple to sort out. He moved the boy's bed from one part of the room to another. 'The ghost was the boy's great-grandfather and the bed was in his way', he explains. The family were never troubled again.

'Eighty per cent of the time the ghosts are members of the family. I tell people that if they want me to get rid of them, I might be throwing their grandmother out of the house. I worry that they might miss her.'

Mr Roberts calls ghosts 'yesterday's people'. His advice is simple. 'You just need to tell them, firmly, to go away and leave you alone.'

VOCABULARY
Phrasal verbs

Go away and leave me alone.

1 Phrasal verbs consist of a verb + adverb/preposition. Some phrasal verbs are literal.

Go away and leave me alone.
Take off your coat and come and **sit down**.

Complete the sentences with a word from the box.

> out (x2)   up   on   back

1 Put _____ something warm. It's cold today.
2 There's some ice-cream in the freezer. Can you get it _____ ?
3 Why are your clothes on the floor? Please pick them _____ .
4 I'm going to take the dog _____ for a walk.
5 When are you going _____ to your country?

Take off your coat and come and sit down.

Do or mime these actions.

> turn round   walk out   try something on   throw something away
> look for something   turn something off   fall over   lie down

2 Some phrasal verbs aren't literal.

'Can you **sort out** this problem?'   The plane **took off**.   I **gave up** my job.

The plane took off.

Do or mime these actions.

> look after a baby   put out a cigarette   look up a word   ask somebody out
> we've run out of milk   my car broke down   Look out!   fill in a form

I gave up my job.

3 Look at the position of the object when it is a pronoun in these sentences.
*Your shoes are dirty. Take **them** off.*   *This jumper looks nice. Can I try **it** on?*

Complete the sentences with phrasal verbs from exercises 1–2. Use pronouns.

1 'Where's my tea?' 'Sorry. I threw _____ . It was cold.'
2 You shouldn't smoke in here. Put _____ .
3 We don't need all these lights on. Turn _____ .
4 Leave little Annie with me. I'll look _____ .
5 I haven't got time to fill in this form. I'll fill _____ later.

your shoes are dirty. Take them off.

4 Complete the sentences with one of these phrasal verbs in the correct form.

> grow up   go out with   fall out with   get on with   look forward to

1 How do you _____ your parents?
2 Do you ever _____ your brothers and sisters?
3 What are you _____ doing on holiday?
4 Are you _____ anyone at the moment?
5 Where did you _____ ? Or have you always lived here?

In pairs, ask and answer the questions about you.

This jumper looks nice. Can I try it on?

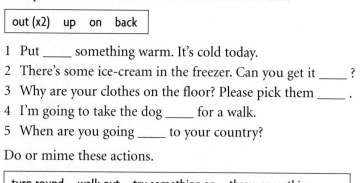

EVERYDAY ENGLISH
Social expressions 2

1 Complete the conversations with the correct expressions.

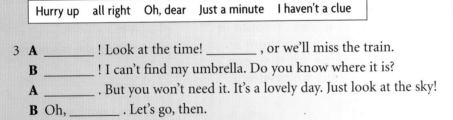

| I'm sorry   Excuse me   of course   Pardon |

1 **A** _____ ! Can I get past?
   B _____ ?
   A Can I get past, please?
   B _____ . I didn't hear you. Yes, _____ .
   A Thanks a lot.

| That's right   Oh, what a pity   Congratulations   Never mind   I hear |

2 **A** _____ you're going to get married soon. _____ !
   B _____ , next July. July 21. Can you come to the wedding?
   A _____ ! That's when we're away on holiday.
   C _____ . We'll send you some wedding cake.
   A That's very kind.

| Hurry up   all right   Oh, dear   Just a minute   I haven't a clue |

3 **A** _____ ! Look at the time! _____ , or we'll miss the train.
   B _____ ! I can't find my umbrella. Do you know where it is?
   A _____ . But you won't need it. It's a lovely day. Just look at the sky!
   B Oh, _____ . Let's go, then.

| Good luck   See you later   Same to you   Good idea   What about you |
| No, of course not |

4 **A** _____ in your exam!
   B _____ . I hope we both pass.
   A Did you go out last night?
   B _____ . I went to bed early. _____ ?
   A Me, too. _____ after the exam. Let's go for a drink.
   B _____ .

2 **T 12.6** Listen and check. Practise the conversations with a partner.

3 Listen to your teacher. Reply using one of the expressions.

13 Earning a living

Present Perfect Continuous · Word formation · Adverbs · Telephoning

STARTER

1 Ask and answer these questions.
2 Ask your teacher the same questions about *teaching* English.

> *How long have you been learning English?*

> *When did you start?*

STREET LIFE
Present Perfect Continuous

1 Read Andy's story.

2 Match the questions a–f on p103 with the answers in the text.

   T 13.1 Listen and check. Finish Andy's answer in question 4.

3 With a partner, cover the questions and practise the conversation. Then cover the answers, and practise again.

GRAMMAR SPOT

1 Which are the questions in the Present Perfect Continuous? What are the other tenses?

2 Look at these two questions.
   How long have you been selling *The Big Issue*?
   How many copies have you sold today?
   Which question asks about the activity of selling?
   Which question asks about the number of magazines sold?

3 Complete these sentences with the Present Perfect Simple or Continuous.
   I _____ (smoke) since I was 16.
   I _____ (smoke) five cigarettes today.

▶▶ **Grammar Reference 13.1 p129**

STREET LIFE

ANDY'S STORY

Andy, 28, from Scotland, used to have his own taxi business. When he lost it, he also lost his home and his family. He now sleeps on the streets in London. *The Big Issue* is a magazine sold by homeless people in Britain. This gives them a small income, so they can begin to find somewhere to live.

1 ☐ _____
  _____?
  For a year. It was very cold at first, but you get used to it.

2 ☐ _____
  _____?
  I came here to look for work, and I never left.

3 ☐ _____
  _____?
  For six months. I'm in Covent Garden seven days a week selling the magazine.

4 ☐ _____
  _____?
  Lots. But I can't stand people who think I drink or take drugs. My problem is I'm homeless. I want a job, but I need somewhere to live before I can get a job. So I need money to get somewhere to live, but …

5 ☐ _____
  _____?
  Usually about fifty.

6 ☐ _____
  _____?
  So far, ten. But it's still early.

a How many copies do you sell a day?

b How long have you been selling *The Big Issue*?

c Have you made many friends?

d How many copies have you sold today?

e How long have you been sleeping on the streets?

f Why did you come to London?

4 Make more questions about Andy.

- How long/trying to find a job?
- How many jobs/had?
- How long/standing here today?
- How/lose your business?
- How long/had your dog?
- Who/best friend?
- Where/meet him/her?
- How long/known each other?

T 13.2 Listen and check.

5 Ask and answer the questions with a partner. Invent Andy's answers.

T 13.3 Listen and compare your answers.

PRACTICE

Discussing grammar

1 Choose the correct tense.

1 How long *have you been living / do you live* in Paris?
2 Anna *has been finding / has found* a good job.
3 Pete and I *have gone out / have been going out* for over six months.
4 I *bought / have bought* a new flat a few months ago.
5 How long *have you had / have you been having* your car?
6 Tom *worked / has been working* as a postman for the past month.
7 I've *written / 've been writing* an essay all day.
8 I've *written / been writing* six pages.

Talking about you

2 Put the verbs in the Present Perfect Simple or Continuous or the Past Simple.

1 How long _____ you _____ (come) to this school?
2 How long _____ you _____ (use) this book?
3 Which book _____ you _____ (have) before this one?
4 How long _____ you _____ (know) your teacher?

What have they been doing?

3 Make a sentence about the people using an idea from the box. Add *because* and say what they've been doing.

He's hot because he's been running.

hot   back hurts   paint on her clothes
dirty hands   no money   tired   eyes hurt
wet   red face

4 Complete these sentences in the Present Perfect Simple about some of the people in exercise 3.

1 He _____ (run) five miles.
2 They _____ (spend) all their money.
3 She _____ (read) five books today.
4 They _____ (play) six games.
5 He _____ (make) a cake and a pie.

Getting information

5 Work with a partner. Your teacher will give you different information about the life and career of Steven Spielberg, the movie director. Ask and answer questions to complete the information.

Student A
Steven Spielberg was born in . . . *(Where?)* He is one of the most successful filmmakers of the late 20th century, and in his career he has earned millions of dollars.

Student B
Steven Spielberg was born in Ohio. He is one of the most successful filmmakers of the late 20th century, and in his career he has earned . . . *(How much?)*

Where was Steven Spielberg born?

He was born in Ohio.

Millions of dollars.

How much has he earned?

VOCABULARY
Word formation

1 These words appeared in the last few units. Complete the charts and mark the stress.

Noun	Verb
death	_die_
waste	_____
_____	be'lieve
_____	'advertise
'promise	_____
_____	feel
ad'vice	_____
_____	de'scribe
in'vention	_____
'government	_____

Noun	Adjective
death	_____
_____	'honest
va'riety	_____
_____	mad
'mystery	_____
_____	'beautiful
_____	'wealthy
suc'cess	_____
_____	'comfortable
peace	_____

2 Complete the sentences with a word from exercise 1.

1 _____ me that you'll always love me.
2 He was taken to hospital by ambulance, but he was _____ on arrival.
3 'Are they _____ ?' 'Yes, they're millionaires.'
   'Where does their money come from?' 'They have a very _____ business.'
4 I love the _____ and quiet of the countryside.
5 I saw an _____ for a job as a waiter.
6 The sofa was so _____ that I fell asleep.
7 I gave the police a _____ of the man who attacked me.
8 I had a few problems, but Bob gave me some good _____ .
9 I was sitting at home when suddenly I had a funny _____ that I wasn't alone.

Adverbs

1 Complete the sentences with the adverbs.

mainly possibly really nearly

1 'Are you going out?' '_____ . I don't know yet.'
2 The exam was _____ difficult. I couldn't do any of it.
3 'How old are you?' 'I'm _____ eight. It's my birthday next week.'
4 I travel a lot in my job, _____ to Europe.

2 Complete the sentences with the adverbs.

seriously exactly carefully fluently

1 I used to speak French _____ , but I've forgotten it now.
2 Please drive _____ . The roads are so dangerous.
3 I have _____ £3.52 to last until the end of the week.
4 There was an accident, but fortunately no one was _____ injured.

READING AND SPEAKING
A funny way to earn a living

1 Play the alphabet game with jobs.

*a*rchitect, *a*ccountant, …
*b*usinessman, *b*ookseller, …

2 What is considered to be a good job in your country? What's an average salary?

3 Look at the pictures and the headlines, and look at the three texts for ten seconds only. Answer the questions.

1 Do they have regular jobs?
2 Do they like their job?
3 Each headline contains one of these words. What's the difference between them?

> life   lively   living

4 Choose one of the texts, and read it more carefully. Answer the questions.

1 Does he/she work indoors or outdoors?
2 How long has he/she been doing this job?
3 What does he/she do in his/her job?
4 What did he/she do before?
5 Does he/she do the same thing every day?
6 How much does he/she earn?
7 Why does he/she like the job?

5 Find two partners who read the other two texts. Compare the three people. Now answer the questions.

1 Who earns the most?
2 Who earns the least?
3 What sort of things has Terry found?
4 Why do Tesco's employ older people?
5 How long has Cathy been flying balloons?
6 What is Terry's philosophy on life?
7 Why didn't Tom phone when he saw the advertisement?
8 How many hours a day does Cathy work?

What do you think?

What is your idea of the best and worst jobs in the world?

Language work

Find five adverbs that end in *-ly* in the text about the beachcomber on p107.

Lively Tom, 69, skates for Tesco
He gets paid for putting on his roller skates

Tom Hopperton is one of 1,200 over-65s working for the supermarket, Tesco. He's been working there for fifteen months. Before that he was a plumber for thirty years.

Tom skates about five miles a day around the store fetching things for customers who realize that they've forgotten something only when they've reached the checkout till. He earns £4.50 an hour.

'I just love the job. I help the customers, so they're usually very nice to me. I've always liked meeting people. And it keeps me fit. I can't sit at home doing nothing. I'd just die. I have to keep busy. Time goes really quickly. Every day is different.'

Tesco's made the decision to employ people of all ages. It sees the advantages of older workers who are more calm and authoritative when they are dealing with customers.

'When I saw this job advertised, I didn't believe they'd give it to me,' says Tom. 'I went in to see them because I thought they would be put off by my age if I just phoned. I wanted them to see that I am very lively for my age.'

Life's a beach

Is it possible to make a living from what you can find on the beach?

For 25 years Terry Cemm was a policeman, but for the last seventeen years he has been walking up and down five miles of beach every day, looking for things that might be useful to someone. Terry's a beachcomber.

Nearly everything in his cottage has come from the sea – chairs, tables, even tins of food. What's the most unusual thing he has ever found? 'A barrel of beer just before Christmas. That was nice,' he remembers. He finds lots of bottles with messages in them, mainly from children. They all get a reply if there's an address in the bottle. Shoes? 'If you find one, you'll find the other the next week,' he says.

But does he really make a living? 'Half a living,' he replies. I barter with a lot of things I find, and I have my police pension. But I don't actually need money. My life is rich in variety.'

Terry seems to be a very happy man. 'You have to find a way to live a simple, honest life. People spend all their lives chasing things they don't really need. There's so much waste.'

'Some people say I'm mad,' says Terry. 'But there are a lot more who'd like to do what I do. Look at me. I've got everything that I could possibly want.'

Flying for a living

Cathy has made a career out of her passion

Cathy Moorhead has only ever had one job. She has never wanted to do anything but be in a hot air balloon, going where the wind takes her, listening to the birds, and watching deer and small animals below her.

And she gets paid for it, about £25,000 a year. 'I've been flying balloons since I was 10, and I have done it professionally for twelve years. I fly between 10 and 20 passengers in different balloons.' The flights usually last an hour, and they go early in the morning or just before sunset. 'The trips are always mystery tours,' she says. 'I never know where we're going to land.'

She starts work about 6 am, and works anything from 15 hours a day to nothing, if the weather is bad. 'We can't fly if it's too windy, if visibility is poor, or if it's raining. The balloon gets too heavy and the passengers get wet.' What's the best thing about the job? 'The job itself. I love being out in the countryside and I hate routines. So this is heaven for me.'

LISTENING AND SPEAKING
Giving news

1 Craig has left home and has just started his first job in advertising. He's on the telephone to his mother.

T 13.4 Listen to his side of the conversation.

Work with a partner and decide if these statements are true (✓) or false (✗).

1 Craig starts work at eight o'clock every morning.
2 His mother is worried that he hasn't been eating well.
3 He goes home immediately after work.
4 Craig's mother has not heard about Tessa before.
5 Craig and Tessa share a flat.
6 Tessa has been working for the advertising agency longer than Craig.
7 Craig's father has been working in Holland.
8 Craig's father has been working hard all day.
9 His mother is coming to London next Thursday.
10 Craig and Tessa are going to cook a meal for his mother.

2 **T 13.4** Listen to Craig again. Your teacher will stop the recording. What do you think his mother said?

3 **T 13.5** Listen to the complete conversation and compare your ideas.

Language work

Read the tapescript on p122. Underline examples of the Present Perfect Simple and Continuous.

Roleplay

1 Read Ruth's diary. Work with a partner. One of you is Ruth. It's Friday evening and you have phoned your friend for a chat.

> *Hi, there. I'm exhausted. I've had a terrible week!*

> *What have you been doing?*

2 Work with a partner. It is Friday evening. One of you has decided to phone the other for a chat. Ask and answer questions about what you've been doing this week.

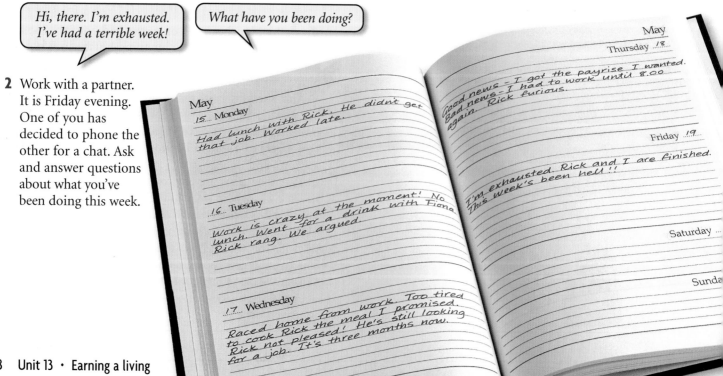

May
15 Monday
Had lunch with Rick. He didn't get that job. Worked late.

16 Tuesday
Work is crazy at the moment! No lunch. Went for a drink with Fiona. Rick rang. We argued.

17 Wednesday
Raced home from work. Too tired to cook Rick the meal I promised. Rick not pleased! He's still looking for a job. It's three months now.

May
Thursday 18
Good news – I got the payrise I wanted. Bad news – I had to work until 8.00 again. Rick furious.

Friday 19
I'm exhausted. Rick and I are finished. This week's been hell!!

Saturday

Sunda

EVERYDAY ENGLISH
Telephoning

1 Practise saying these telephone numbers.

020 7927 4863   01923 272994   0797 0800 994   633488
061 44 501277   07880 705024

T 13.6 Listen and check.

2 **T 13.7** Listen to some phone numbers in American English. What differences are there between British and American English?

3 **T 13.8** Listen to three phone conversations and decide:

- who is speaking to who.
- what about.
- how well they know each other.

> **!** 1 Look at these telephone expressions.
> Who's speaking?
> Is that Mike?
> This is John./It's John.
> (NOT ~~Here is~~ John, or ~~I'm~~ John.)
>
> 2 Complete these expressions from the telephone conversations.
> Could I _____ Ann Baker?
> I _____ he's out at the moment.
> Can I take a _____ ?
> I'll _____ later.
>
> 3 What do these mean?
> Hold on. I'll connect you.
> Speaking.

4 Look at the tapescript on p122. Practise the conversations with a partner.

5 Your teacher will give you a role card. Prepare what you are going to say alone, then be ready to make a call or answer the phone.

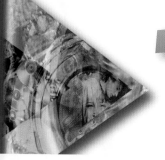

14 Love you and leave you

Past Perfect · Reported statements · Saying goodbye

STARTER

Match the lines about John and Mary.

They met each other	every week.
They've known each other	when they met.
They see each other	for a long time.
They were living in New York	a long time ago.
They had never been to New York	before.

A LOVE STORY
Past Perfect

1 Texts **A** and **B** are summaries of a magazine love story. Read and compare them.

One Short Hot Summer
by Carmen Day

A *The story so far ...*

Saskia met Bradley at a party one Saturday night in June. They fell in love and got married the following Saturday. After the wedding, Bradley moved into Saskia's flat. Saskia rang her parents and told them that she was married. They were furious.

Unfortunately, after a few months, Bradley began to behave very strangely and his marriage to Saskia started to go wrong ...

B *The story so far ...*

Saskia and Bradley got married one Saturday in June. They had met only one week earlier at a party and had fallen in love. After the wedding, Saskia rang her parents and told them that she was married, and that Bradley had moved into her flat. They were furious.

Unfortunately, after a few months, their marriage started to go wrong. Bradley had begun to behave very strangely ...

2 **T 14.1** Read and listen to text **B** on p110 and underline all the examples of the Past Perfect. Read the text aloud and pay attention to contracted forms.

3 Are the following statements about Saskia and Bradley true (✔) or false (✗)? Correct the false ones.

1 When Saskia and Bradley got married, they had known each other for a year.
2 When Saskia told her parents about the wedding, Bradley had already moved into her flat.
3 Her parents were angry because she hadn't phoned them for a long time.
4 The marriage started to go wrong, and then Bradley began to behave very strangely.

PRACTICE
Speaking

1 The story continues. Work with a partner. Tell the story in the order of the pictures.

1   On Friday evening when Bradley returned from work, he … his suitcase.

2   Then he …

3   and …

4   Saskia … home.

2 Which of these sentences is true? Explain why.

	was packing.
When Saskia arrived home, Bradley	packed.
	had packed.

3 Tell the story again, but begin at picture 4.
   When Saskia arrived home, Bradley …

Grammar and pronunciation

4 Make sentences from the chart below.

I	was in a mess			had	fallen over playing football.
Our teacher	hurt		I		done the homework.
My leg	died	because			passed all my exams.
The plants	was delighted				had a party the night before.
The house	was angry		we		forgotten to water them.
	was hungry			hadn't	had a busy day.
	went to bed early				had any breakfast.

T 14.2 Listen and check. Practice saying the sentences.

5 The *had* in the Past Perfect tense is often contracted.

I'd passed my exams. (The *'d* is sometimes difficult to hear.)

(*'d* is also the contracted form of *would*: *I'd like to come.*)

T 14.3 Listen to the sentences. Put a tick (✔) if the sentence contains *had*. Put a cross (✗) if it doesn't.

1 ☐   2 ☐   3 ☐   4 ☐   5 ☐   6 ☐   7 ☐   8 ☐   9 ☐   10 ☐

6 Put the verbs into the correct tense, Past Simple or Past Perfect.

The story continues ...

Saskia (1) _____ (read) Bradley's letter and then she (2)_____ (walk) slowly into the kitchen.

Earlier that day she (3) _____ (buy) his favourite food for dinner, now she (4) _____ (throw) it into the rubbish bin. Why (5)_____ he _____ (do) this to her? She remembered how happy they (6) _____ (be) in the beginning. They (7) _____ (laugh) a lot then. Saskia (8) _____ (feel) desperate.

One hour later the phone (9)_____ (ring) in the flat ...

7 Read the end of the story. What happened before? Write your ideas in groups.

The end of the story

Bradley took Saskia in his arms and said, 'Forgive me, my darling. I'm so happy we're together again – this time it's forever!'

WHAT DID SHE SAY?
Reported statements

1 **T 14.4** Listen and complete what Mary says about John in **A**.

A What does Mary say?
'I _____ John very much.'
'We _____ six months ago.'
'I _____ in love before.'
'We _____ very happy.'
'I _____ him forever.'
'I _____ him this evening.

2 **T 14.5** Read and listen to **B**.

B What did Mary tell you?
She told me/said that . . .
she loved John very much.
they had met six months ago.
she had never been in love before.
they were very happy.
she would love him forever.
she was seeing him that evening.

GRAMMAR SPOT

1 **A** is direct speech. **B** is reported speech. What are the tense changes from direct to reported speech?

2 How are *say* and *tell* used to introduce reported speech?

▶▶▶ **Grammar Reference 14.2 p129**

3 Practise the sentences using contracted forms where possible.

PRACTICE

An interview

1 **T 14.6** Listen to an interview with the writer Carmen Day, who wrote *One Short Hot Summer*.

2 Complete this report of the interview with the correct verb forms.

Carmen Day –
romantic novelist

In an interview Carmen said she (1) **had written** another romantic novel because she (2) _____ romantic fiction easy to write, but that her next novel (3) _____ "something different, possibly a detective story.

Carmen said that the character of Bradley (4) _____ on ¹⁹ her first husband, Clive Maingay, the actor, who (5) _____ ²⁵ her very unhappy. But she added that she (6) _____ ³³ now married to Tony Marsh, the politician. She said that they (7) _____ married for nearly ten years and that they ⁴⁴ (8) _____ very happy together.

She told me that she (9) _____ now _____ ⁵⁸ five novels and also that she (10) _____ three stories for ¹⁰⁴ children. She said she (11) _____ never stop writing, not ¹¹⁰ even when she (12) _____ an old lady.

T 14.7 Listen and check.

Check it

3 Report these statements.
1 'I like Anna,' said Jim.
2 'I'm staying with my aunt,' said Anna.
3 'Mr Walker phoned before lunch,' Sue said.
   'He didn't leave a message,' she added.
4 'I don't think it'll rain,' said Ken.
5 'Ken's gone home,' Sue said.
   'He went early,' she added.
6 'I'll ring you this evening,' Anna told Jim.

READING AND SPEAKING
The tale of two silent brothers

1 Sometimes in families there are arguments and family members don't speak to each other for a long time. Has this ever happened to anyone you know?

2 You are going to read about two brothers who didn't speak to each other for many years. These expressions are in the text. Match the verbs and phrases.

get	a bachelor all his life
make	a coin
have	revenge
see	a will
remain	a quarrel
toss	and make up
kiss	a solicitor about something

3 Read the first part of the story.

PART ONE | A death in the family

There were once two brothers, John and Robert Hessian. John was 52 years old, Robert 49. They had never married and they lived together in a house in Oldcastle in the north of England. They lived together, they ate meals together but they never spoke a single word to each other. They hadn't spoken to each other for ten years, ever since they had had a quarrel. Whenever they wanted to communicate they wrote notes.

One evening the brothers were sitting together after supper. They were both wearing black because their older sister, Mary, had recently died. John wrote a note to Robert: *Mr Liversage is coming to visit.* (Mr Liversage was their solicitor.)
Robert wrote: *Why?*
John wrote: *I don't know. He phoned and said that he wanted to see us.*
At that moment there was a knock at the door. It was the solicitor, Mr Powell Liversage. He had been to school with the brothers and was an old friend. He too was unmarried.
'How are you, Powell?' asked Robert.
'Very well,' he replied. 'I've come to tell you about your sister's will. Did you know that she had left a will?'
'No,' answered John and Robert together. 'How much did she leave?'
'£12,000. But let me read you the will.'

What do you think?

Discuss these questions with a partner before you read part two.

Why do you think the brothers quarrelled? Do you think they quarrelled about:

• money?   • the house?   • a woman?

What do you think is in the will? Do you think:

• the sister leaves the brothers £6,000 each?
• she leaves all the money to one brother? Which one?
• she leaves them the money on certain conditions? What conditions?

4 Read part two and find out if your ideas are correct.

PART TWO | The will

Mr Liversage took the will out of his pocket and began to read.

Last Will and Testament of Mary Hessian

To my dear brothers John and Robert:

You have both behaved very stupidly. I have never understood why you quarrelled about Annie Emery. You have been cruel and unfair to poor Annie. She has waited ten years for one of you. So, John, if you marry Annie, I'll give all my money to you. And Robert, if you marry her, I'll give it to you. And, if neither of you marries her, all my money will go to Annie, herself.

Your ever-loving sister

Mary

What do you think?

Discuss these questions as a class before you read part three.

- What do you think will happen?
- What will John and Robert do?
- Who will marry Annie?

5 Read part three and find out if your ideas are correct.

PART THREE | To marry or not to marry?

The two brothers sat and thought for a long time. Ten years ago when Annie was a young woman of 27, both John and Robert had been in love with her. They had had a violent quarrel and some terrible things were said. Afterwards they had both wanted to make up and be friends again but by this time they had stopped speaking to each other, so neither of them learned that the other had decided not to marry Annie.

At two o'clock in the morning John spoke: 'Why don't we toss a coin for Annie? Heads or tails?'

'Tails,' said Robert. But it was heads. The next evening John went round to Annie's house. Powell Liversage was just leaving when he arrived.

So in the end neither brother married Annie. They are still bachelors to this day, but at least they are now talking to each other again. And Annie? Well, she got her revenge and now she's very happily married.

ADAPTED FROM A STORY BY ARNOLD BENNET

What do you think?

Discuss these questions with a partner. Then tell the class your ideas.

- What happened when John went to Annie's house?
- Why didn't Annie marry either brother?
- Who did she marry?
- Who got the money?

Your teacher will tell you what actually happened.

Language work

Complete the sentences using the Past Perfect.

1 John and Robert didn't speak to each other because …
2 They were wearing black because …
3 They didn't know that their sister …
4 Mary said in her will that …
5 When Annie was 27, both brothers …
6 Annie told John that she wouldn't marry him or his brother because …

LISTENING AND VOCABULARY
Talk to me

1 [T 14.8] Close your books and your eyes and listen to a song. What is it about?

2 Work with a partner. Complete the song, choosing the best word on the right for each line.

Talk to me by Bruce Springsteen

Well, every night I see a _____ up in your window
But every night you won't _____ the door
But although you won't _____ let me in
From the street I can see your _____ sitting close to him

light	man
come to	answer
never	ever
silhouette	shadow

What must I do?
What does it take
To get you to

Talk to me
Until the night is over
Talk to me
Well until the night is over, yeah yeah yeah
I got a full week's _____
And baby I've been working hard _____ day
I'm not _____ for the world, you see
I'm just asking, girl
Talk to me

pay	stay
all	each
asking	looking

Well late at night I hear music that
    you're playing _____ and low
Yes and late at night I see the two of
    you _____, so close
I don't understand darling, what was
    my _____?
Why am I down here below _____
    you're up there with him?

soft	loud
sitting	swaying
mistake	sin
while	when

What did I do?
What did I say?
What must I pay
To get you to
Talk to me

3 [T 14.8] Listen again and check.

EVERYDAY ENGLISH

Saying goodbye

1 Match the sentences with the correct photos.

1 **c** 'Goodbye! Have a safe journey. Send us a postcard!'
2 ☐ 'Goodbye. Thank you for a lovely evening.' 'You must come to us next time.'
3 ☐ 'Goodbye. It has been most interesting talking to you. We'll let you know by post.'
4 ☐ 'Bye! See you later. Are you doing anything tonight?'
5 ☐ 'Bye-bye! Thank you very much for having me.'
6 ☐ 'Goodbye. Here's my number. Please get in touch if you have any problems with it.'
7 ☐ 'Goodbye! Drive carefully and call us when you get there!'
8 ☐ 'Goodbye! Good luck in the future. I've really enjoyed our lessons together!'

2 **T 14.9** Listen and check. Practise saying the sentences.

3 Make more conversations for these situations:

• parents saying goodbye to son/daughter leaving home to share a flat with friends
• saying goodbye to friends after spending a holiday with them
• saying goodbye to your teacher/boss after finishing school/work on Friday
• saying goodbye to teachers/schoolfriends when you leave school

Tapescripts

Unit 8

T 8.1 Steven's job

I = Interviewer S = Steven

I What sort of hours do you work, Steven?
S Well, I have to work very long hours, about eleven hours a day.
I What time do you start?
S I work nine till three, then I start again at five thirty and work until eleven. Six days a week. So I have to work very unsocial hours.
I And do you have to work at the weekend?
S Oh, yes. That's our busiest time. I get Wednesdays off.
I What are some of the things you have to do, and some of the things you don't have to do?
S Er … I don't have to do the washing-up, so that's good! I have to wear white, and I have to be very careful about hygiene. Everything in the kitchen has to be totally clean.
I What's hard about the job?
S You're standing up all the time. When we're busy, people get angry and shout, but that's normal.
I How did you learn the profession?
S Well, I did a two-year course at college. In the first year we had to learn the basics, and then we had to take exams.
I Was it easy to find a job?
S I wrote to about six hotels, and one of them gave me my first job, so I didn't have to wait too long.
I And what are the secrets of being good at your job?
S Attention to detail. You have to love it. You have to be passionate about it.
I And what are your plans for the future?
S I want to have my own place. When the time's right.

T 8.2

1 I have a good job.
   I have to work hard.
2 He has a nice car.
   She has to get up early.
3 I had a good time.
   I had to take exams.

T 8.3

1 'I'm working 16 hours a day'.
   'I think you should talk to your boss.'
2 'I can't sleep.'
   'You shouldn't drink coffee at night.'
3 'My ex-boyfriend's getting married.'
   'I don't think you should go to the wedding.'
4 'I've had a terrible toothache for weeks.'
   'You must go to the dentist!'

T 8.4 Holidays in January

1 **Silvia**
   In January the weather is wonderful. It's the most perfect time of year, not too hot, not too cold, but the temperature can change a lot in just one day. It can go from quite chilly to very warm, so you should perhaps bring a jacket but you don't need any thick winter clothes. The capital city is the most populated city in the world and there are lots of things to see and do there. We have lots of very old, historic buildings. We are very proud of our history, with Mayan and Aztec temples. But you should also go to the coast. We have beautiful beaches. Perhaps you've heard of Acapulco.
   You don't need a lot of money to enjoy your holiday. There are lots of good cheap hotels and restaurants, and of course you must visit the markets. You can buy all kinds of pottery and things quite cheaply, and don't forget our wonderful fruit and vegetables. We have one hundred different kinds of pepper. You should try tacos, which are a kind of bread filled with meat, beans, and salad. And our beer is very good, especially if you add lemon and salt. Or, of course, you can always drink *tequila*.

2 **Fatima**
   It's usually quite mild in January, and it doesn't often rain, so you don't have to bring warm clothes. But you'll need a light coat or a jumper because it can get cool in the evenings.
   There is so much to see and do. We have some wonderful museums, especially the museum of Islamic Art and the mosques are beautiful, but of course what everyone wants to see is the Pyramids. You must visit the pyramids. Go either early in the morning or late in the afternoon, the light is much better then. And if you have time you should take a cruise down the Nile, that's really interesting, you can visit all sorts of places that are difficult to get to by land.
   The best place to try local food is in the city centre. You should try *koftas* and *kebabs*, which are made of meat, usually lamb. You should also try *falafel*, which is a kind of ball made of beans mixed with herbs, it's fried until it's crispy. It's delicious. One of the nicest things to drink is tea, mint tea. It's especially good if the weather is very hot, it's really refreshing.

3 **Karl**
   Well, of course in January in my country it can be very cold, with lots of snow everywhere, so you must bring lots of warm clothes, coats and woolly hats, and, if you can, snow boots.
   Many people go skiing in the mountains at the weekends and when you are up so high and the sky is blue, the sun can feel really quite hot - warm enough to have lunch outside. You can even sunbathe, so you should bring sun cream! But you don't have to go skiing, there are lots of other things to do and see. A lot of our towns are very pretty. They look exactly the same today as they did four hundred years ago. And we have beautiful lakes. If the weather's fine you can go for a boat trip and you can get really wonderful views of the mountains all around, from Lake Geneva you can sometimes see as far as Mont Blanc.
   The food you must try is *fondue* , which is cheese melted in a pot. You put pieces of bread on long forks to get it out. Also you could try *rösti* made with potatoes and cream – mmm! They're both delicious.

T 8.5

1 Children always need the support of their parents, whether they're four or 24. I think you should pay for him to get some qualifications, and when he's ready, you should help him to find somewhere to live. Meanwhile, you've got to give him all the love that he needs.
   Jenny Torr
   Brighton

2 I decided to give it all up and change my life dramatically three years ago. Since then, I have had the most exciting three years of my life. It can be scary, but if you don't do it, you won't know what you've missed. I don't think she should worry. Go for it.
   Mike Garfield
   Manchester

3 He's using you. I think you should tell him to leave home. It's time for him to go. Twenty-four is too old to be living with his parents. He's got to take responsibility for himself. And you must tell the police about his drug-taking. Sometimes you have to be cruel to be kind.
   Tony Palmer
   Harrow

4 Why should he accept it? He isn't their slave, they don't own him. And I too can't stand the way people use their mobiles in restaurants, on trains and buses. They think that the people around them are invisible and can't hear. It is so rude.
   Jane Sands
   London

5 I think she should be very careful before she gives up her job and goes to live abroad. Does she think that the sun will always shine? If there is something in her life that makes her unhappy now, this will follow her. She should take her time before making a decision.
   Nigella Lawnes
   Bristol

6 He must keep it! He should have a word with his company and come to an arrangement with them. Why can't he turn it off sometimes? Mobile phones are great, and if he's got one for free, he's very lucky. They are one of the best inventions ever.
   Pete Hardcastle
   Birmingham

T 8.6

alarm clock	hairdrier
car park	sunset
traffic lights	earring
credit card	signpost
ice-cream	bookcase
sunglasses	rush hour
timetable	cigarette lighter
raincoat	earthquake

D = Doctor   M = Manuel

D Hello. Come and sit down. What seems to be the matter?

M Well, I haven't felt very well for a few days. I've got a bit of a temperature, and I just feel terrible. I've got stomach ache as well.

D Have you felt sick?

M I've been sick a few times.

D Mm. Let me have a look at you. Your glands aren't swollen. Have you got a sore throat?

M No, I haven't.

D Have you had diarrhoea at all?

M Yes, I have, actually.

D Have you had anything to eat recently which might have disagreed with you?

M No, I don't think … Oh! I went to a barbecue a few days ago and the chicken wasn't properly cooked.

D It could be that, or just something that was left out of the fridge for too long.

M Yes, I started being ill that night.

D Well, you should have a day or two in bed, and I'll give you something that will look after the stomach ache and diarrhoea. Drink plenty of liquids, and just take things easy for a while. I'll write you a prescription.

M Thank you. Do I have to pay you?

D No, no. Seeing me is free, but you'll have to pay for the prescription. It's £6.

M Right. Thanks very much. Goodbye.

D Bye-bye.

Unit 9

T 9.1

1 We're travelling round the world before we go to university.

2 We're going to leave as soon as we have enough money.

3 When we're in Australia, we're going to learn to scuba dive on the Great Barrier Reef.

4 If we get ill, we'll look after each other.

5 After we leave Australia, we're going to the USA.

6 We can stay with my American cousins while we're in Los Angeles.

7 Our parents will be worried if we don't keep in touch.

8 We'll stay in the States until our visa runs out.

T 9.2

1 When I get home, I'm going to have a bath.

2 As soon as this lesson finishes, I'm going home.

3 If I win, I'll buy a new car.

4 After I leave school, I want to go to college.

5 While I'm in New York, I'll do some shopping.

6 I'm going to travel the world before I get too old.

T 9.3

P = Paul   M = Mary

P Bye, darling. Have a good trip to New York.

M Thanks. I'll ring you as soon as I arrive at the hotel.

P Fine. Remember I'm going out with Henry tonight.

M Well, if you're out when I ring, I'll leave a

message on the answer phone, so you'll know I've arrived safely.

P Great. What time do you expect you'll be there?

M If the plane arrives on time, I'll be at the hotel about 10.00.

P All right. Give me a ring as soon as you know the time of your flight back, and I'll pick you up at the airport.

M Thanks, darling. Don't forget to water the plants while I'm away.

P Don't worry. I won't. Bye!

T 9.4   An interview with Michio Kaku

I = Interviewer MK = Michio Kaku

I Are you optimistic about the future?

MK Generally, yeah. If we go back to 1900, most Americans didn't live after the age of 50. Since then we've had improvements in healthcare and technology. There's no reason why these won't continue far into the 21st century.

I Are we ready for the changes that will come?

MK Changes are already happening. The future is here now. We have DNA, microchips, the Internet. Some people's reaction is to say 'We're too old, we don't understand new technology.' My reaction is to say 'We must educate people to use new technology now.'

I Is world population going to be a big problem?

MK Yes and no. I think that world population will stop increasing as we all get richer. If you are part of the middle class, you don't want or need twelve children.

I What will happen to people who don't have computers?

MK Everyone will have computers. The Internet will be free and available to everyone.

I Will there be a world government?

MK Very probably. We will have to manage the world and its resources on a global level, because countries alone are too small. We already have a world language called English, and there is the beginning of a world telephone system, and that's called the Internet.

I Will we have control of everything?

MK I think we'll learn to control the weather, volcanoes and earthquakes. Illness won't exist. We will grow new livers, kidneys, hearts, and lungs like spare parts for a car. People will live till about 130 or 150. For two thousand years we have tried to understand our environment. Now we will begin to control it.

I What are your reasons for pessimism?

MK People will still fundamentally be the same, with all their intelligence and stupidity. There will still be cruel people, people who want to fight wars against other races and religions, people who don't see that we have to look after our forests, our oceans, our atmosphere, people who think that money is everything. We will have the technology. The question is, will we have the wisdom to use the technology to our advantage?

T 9.5

1 I did some shopping while I was in town. I bought myself a new jumper.

2 'I don't know if I love Tom or Henry.'

'Make up your mind. You can't marry both of them.'

3 Bye-bye! See you soon. Take care of yourself.

4 Aachoo! Oh dear. I think I'm getting a cold.

5 'Are the doors locked?'
'I think so, but I'll just make sure.'

T 9.6

R = Receptionist   C = Client

R Hello, the Grand Hotel. Cathy speaking. How can I help you?

C I'd like to make a reservation, please.

R Certainly. When is it for?

C It's for two nights, the thirteenth and the fourteenth of this month.

R And do you want a single or a double room?

C A single, please.

R OK. Yes, that's fine. I have a room for you. And your name is?

C Robert Palmer. Can you tell me how much it is?

R Yes. That's £95 a night. Can I have a credit card number, please?

C Yes, sure. It's a Visa. 4929 7983 0621 8849.

R Thank you. And could I have a phone number?

C Uh huh. 01727 489962.

R That's fine. We look forward to seeing you on the thirteenth. Bye-bye.

C Thanks a lot. Goodbye.

Unit 10

T 10.1   Don't look down

Paul Lay dances with death in the mountains of southern Spain

I have always enjoyed walking. When I was a boy, I used to go walking at weekends with my father. We went camping and climbing together.

I try to visit a new place every year. Last year I decided to walk a path in Spain called *El Camino del Rey*, which means the King's Way. It is one of the highest and most dangerous footpaths in Europe. It used to be very safe, but now it is falling down.

I took a train to the village of El Chorro and started to walk towards the mountains. I was very excited.

Then the adventure began. The path was about three feet wide and there were holes in it. It used to have a handrail, but not any more. I didn't know what to do – should I go on my hands and knees, or stand up? I decided to stand up and walk very slowly. At times the path was only as wide as my two boots. I stopped to have a rest, but there was nowhere to sit.

I began to feel very frightened. It was impossible to look down or look up. I was concentrating so hard that my body started aching. There was no thrill of danger, no enjoyment of the view. I thought I was going to die.

I finally managed to get to the end. I was shaking, and I was covered in sweat from heat and fear. I fell to the ground, exhausted.

T 10.2

1 Now I usually go shopping on Saturday, and on Sunday morning I play tennis. When I was a child, I used to go to school on Saturday morning. On Sunday all the family used to get together for Sunday lunch.

2 In the evening I used to watch TV and do my homework. Now I read, or go out with friends.

3 We go to a hotel somewhere hot and just do nothing. When I was young, we used to go camping in Europe. We went everywhere – France, Italy, Austria, Germany.

4 I was very sporty. I used to play everything. Rugby, tennis, swimming, hockey. Now I just play tennis. Oh, and walk the dog!

5 I like documentaries and sport. When I was a kid, I used to like cartoons, comedies, action films, you know, like James Bond.

6 I liked all the things that kids like. Beans, pizza, fizzy drinks. I used to love chips. Still do. Now I eat everything. Except peppers. Really don't like peppers.

T 10.3

1 'I'm hungry. I need something to eat.'
'Have a sandwich.'

2 'I'm going to a posh party, but I don't know what to wear.'
'I think you should wear your black dress.'

3 'My CD player's broken. Can you show me how to repair it?'
'I'm sorry. I haven't a clue.'

4 'Don't talk to me. I have nothing to say to you.'
'Oh, dear! What have I done wrong?'

5 'Do I turn left or right? I don't know where to go.'
'Go straight on.'

6 'I'm bored. I haven't got anything to do.'
'Why don't you read the dictionary?'

7 'Can you get some meat?'
'Sure. Tell me how much to buy.'
'A kilo.'

8 'I feel lonely. I need somebody to talk to.'
'Come and talk to me. I'm not doing anything.'

T 10.4

frightened	terrified
excited	bored
surprised	exhausted

T 10.5

1 I met a famous film star today.
2 I spent four hours going round a museum.
3 I haven't heard from my parents for two months.
4 Wow, Maria! What are you doing here?
5 I failed my exam. I worked …
6 A man started to follow me home last night.
7 My computer's broken, and …

T 10.6 It was just a joke

I = Interviewer J = Jamie

I So you decided to kidnap this boy, Tom, for his eighteenth birthday?

J Yeah, just for a joke. We wanted to give him a real scare.

I So how did you organize it?

J About eight of us planned it. Tom thought he was going round to Richard's house, and Dave was driving him there. They came to a place which is quite dark, and there in the middle of the road was this body, this … dead body.

I And this was one of you?

J Yeah, it was Andrew. Dave stopped the car and got out, and then said to Tom, 'Hey, Tom, come and help. This looks really serious.' So Tom got out. I was hiding behind a tree, and I jumped on him. There were about six of us, all dressed in black with balaclavas on our heads. And I had this gun, well, a toy gun, and I put it in his face and started screaming at him to lie on the ground. Then we tied him up, put a blindfold on him, and threw him in the back of the car.

I Did anyone see you doing this?

J Well, yeah, but I'll tell you about that later.

I And how was Tom? Wasn't he terrified?

J Yeah, it was all so real. Tom started to say things like 'Please, I haven't seen your faces. Please let me go.' We were all so worried … you know, that it was getting too real, but we couldn't stop. 'Please,' he said, 'don't kill me!' Anyway, we got him to Richard's house and put him in a room with just a chair in the middle and all these lights pointing at him, so we could see him but he couldn't see us, and then we all started singing Happy Birthday.

I That's amazing!

J Tom tried to say that he knew it was us from the start, but that's just not true. He was so terrified.

I So what about these people who saw the kidnap?

J Well, someone saw what was happening from a bedroom window and called the police, and soon there were police cars and armed police everywhere, dogs, and a police helicopter all looking for terrorists. And that was us!

I And they found you?

J We were driving past later that evening, and the police were stopping everyone and asking if they knew anything about a kidnap, and we had to confess that it was just a joke.

I Weren't they angry with you for wasting so much police time?

J Yeah, well. We're still waiting to hear if we're going to be taken to court.

I And has Tom forgiven you?

J Oh, yeah. He'll never forget his eighteenth birthday, though.

T 10.7 see p85

T 10.8

1 Their house is such a mess! I don't know how they live in it.
2 There were so many people at the party! There was nowhere to dance.
3 I'm so hungry! I could eat a horse.
4 Jane and Pete are such nice people! But I can't stand their kids.
5 I've spent so much money this week! I don't know where it's all gone.
6 A present! For me? You're so kind! You really didn't have to.
7 We've had such a nice time! Thank you so much for inviting us.

8 Molly's such a clever dog! She understands every word I say.

Unit 11

T 11.1 Questions and answers

1 When was the first hamburger made?
In 1895.
2 When was the first McDonald's opened?
In 1948.
3 Where were the first hamburgers made?
In Connecticut.
4 Who were they made by?
Louis Lassen.
5 Why were they called hamburgers?
Because the recipe came from Hamburg.
6 How many McDonald's restaurants have been opened since 1948?
25,000.
7 How many hamburgers are eaten every day?
35 million.

T 11.2

1 A Are Coca-Cola and hamburgers sold *only* in America?
B No, they aren't. They're sold all over the world.

2 A Was Coca-Cola invented by Louis Lassen?
B No, it wasn't. It was invented by John Pemberton.

3 A Were the first hamburgers made in 1948?
B No, they weren't. They were made in 1895.

4 A Was the first McDonald's restaurant opened in New York?
B No, it wasn't. It was opened in San Bernadino, in California.

5 A Have 2,500 restaurants now been opened worldwide?
B No, not 2,500. 25,000 have been opened worldwide.

T 11.3 The history of chewing gum

P = Presenter I = Interviewer
LW = Leanne Ward, chewing gum expert
AB = Interviewees

Part one

P Today in Worldly Wise, the world's most common habit … .
Yes, chewing gum. We chew 100,000 tons of it every year but how many of us actually know what it's made of?

I Excuse me, I see you're chewing gum …

A Yeah.

I Have you got any idea what it's made of?

A Nah – no idea. Never thought about it.

I Have *you* any idea what chewing gum is made of?

B … Er no, not a clue. Rubber maybe?

I And do you have any idea who invented it?

A The Americans?

B Yeah – sure – I reckon it was invented in America, yeah.

P Well no. It wasn't the Americans who invented chewing gum. It was the Swedes. The Swedes, I hear you say? But listen to Leanne Ward, a chewing gum expert.

LW The history of chewing goes back thousands of years. In Sweden in 1993, the skeleton of a teenager was found, he was nine thousand years old. And in his mouth was a gum made of tree sap and sweetened with honey – the first known chewing gum.

P   It seems we've always chewed things of no real food value. Babies are born wanting to chew. Everything goes straight into their mouths. So why do we chew? Here's Leanne again.

LW We chew to clean our teeth and freshen our breath but also because we just like chewing. The ancient Greeks chewed a gum called *mastica*, which is a type of tree sap. They thought it was good for their health and women really enjoyed chewing it as a way to sweeten their breath. Then in the first century AD we know that the Mayan Indians in South America liked to chew a tree sap, called *chiclay*. They wrapped it in leaves and put it in their mouths so this was, if you like, the first packet of chewing gum. The American Indians also chewed tree sap – they gave it to the English when they arrived, but it wasn't until a few hundred years after, that it became really popular in America.

T 11.4   Part two

P   The history of modern chewing gum begins in 19th century America. In 1892 a clever young salesman called William Wrigley decided that chewing gum was the thing of the future. Wrigley was a business genius. He was the first to use advertising to sell in a big way. Here's Leanne.

LW William Wrigley was really an advertising genius. He hired hundreds of pretty girls, who he called 'the Wrigley girls'. They walked up and down the streets of Chicago and New York City handing out free gum. Millions of pieces were given away. He also had huge electric signs and billboards – one billboard was a mile long, it ran along the side of the train track. So with all this, chewing gum became very popular all over the USA.

P   So how did the world get to know and love chewing gum? Leanne again.

LW Well, during the Second World War American soldiers were given Wrigley gum to help them relax. In 1944 *all* gum production went to the US Army and they took their gum overseas and gave it to children. Soon they were followed everywhere by the cry: 'Got any gum, chum?'.

P   And so the popularity of gum spread to other countries. After the war sales of gum exploded worldwide. Chewing gum was even taken into space by the first astronauts. So what exactly *is* it made of?

LW Well, the strangest thing about gum today is that nobody knows what it's made of. Nobody will tell you. The chewing gum industry keeps the recipe top secret.

T 11.5

1   'Are we nearly there yet, Dad?'
    'No. It's miles to go, but we'll stop soon and have something to eat.'
    'All right. I need the toilet, anyway.'
2   'How much is it to send this letter to Australia?'
    'Give it to me and I'll weigh it. That's … £1.20.'
    'OK. That's fine. And a book of ten first-class stamps, please.'

'All right.'
3   'Hi. Can I pay for my petrol, please?'
    'Which pump?'
    'Er … pump number … five.'
    'Forty-one pounds 78p, please.'
4   The 7.56 from Bristol is now arriving at platform 4. Virgin Rail would like to apologize for the late arrival of this service. This was due to circumstances beyond our control.
5   'A vodka and orange, please.'
    'How old are you?'
    'Eighteen.'
    'Hmm. Have you got any identification on you?'
    'No.'

Unit 12

T 12.1

If I were a princess, I'd live in a palace. I'd have servants to look after me. My Mum would be Queen, and she wouldn't work. I wouldn't go to school. I'd have a private teacher. I'd ride a white horse, and I'd wear a long dress. I could have all the sweets I wanted.

T 12.2   see p96

T 12.3

1   'I have no money. What am I going to do?'
    'If I were you, I'd try to spend less.'
    'What do you mean?'
    'Well, you buy a lot of clothes, designer clothes. Stop buying such expensive clothes.'
    'But I like them!'
2   'My hair's awful. I can't do anything with it.'
    'It's not that bad.'
    'It is, really. Just look at it.'
    'Well, if I were you, I'd try that new hairdresser, Antonio. He's supposed to be very good, and not that expensive.'
    'Mmm. OK, I'll try it. Thanks.'
3   'I've got toothache.'
    'Have you seen a dentist?'
    'No.'
    'Well, if I were you, I'd make an appointment right now.'
4   'I've had a row with my boyfriend.'
    'What about?'
    'Oh, the usual thing. He gets jealous if I just look at another boy.'
    'And did you?'
    'No, of course not!'
    'Well, if I were you, I'd love him and leave him. He won't ever change, you know.'
    'Oh, I couldn't do that.'
5   'My car won't start in the morning.'
    'If I were you, I'd buy a new one. Yours is so old.'
    'I know it's old, but I can't afford a new one.'
    'Well, take it to a garage. Let them have a look at it.'
    'All right.'
6   'My neighbours make a lot of noise.'
    'Do they? That's awful.'
    'Mmm. We can't get to sleep at night.'
    'Have you spoken to them about this?'
    'No, we're too frightened.'
    'If I were you, I'd invite them round to your flat for coffee and say that you're having

problems.'
    'That's probably a good idea. I'm not sure they'll come, but I'll try it.'

T 12.4

Ruth
I'm having a holiday in Italy for a couple of weeks, staying in a villa in Tuscany. Then I'm going to look for a job. I want to work in the media – advertising or the BBC would be perfect.
    My sister and I are going to buy a flat together, somewhere central, so we'll have to start looking soon. I'm very excited about the future. And I'm also highly ambitious!

Henry
I'm not sure yet. Some friends have invited me to go to Long Island with them, so I might go to America. I'll have to earn some money, so I might work in a restaurant for a bit.
    I don't know what I want to do. I love France, so I might live in Paris for a while. I could earn some money painting portraits in Montmartre. Who knows? I might meet a beautiful French girl and fall in love! Wouldn't that be wonderful!

T 12.5

I = Interviewer   A = Alice Lester
I   When did you first hear these voices, Alice?
A   Well, I was at home, sitting and reading.
I   And what did they say?
A   The first time, there was just one voice. It said, 'Don't be afraid, I just want to help you.'
I   But it didn't say how it wanted to help you?
A   No, it didn't. It just went away.
I   And what about the second time?
A   It was while I was away on holiday, but this time there were two voices. They told me to go back home immediately, because there was something wrong with me.
I   So is that what you did?
A   Yes. And when I was back in London, the voices gave me an address to go to.
I   And what was the address?
A   Well, now it starts to get very strange. The address was the brain scan department of St Mary's Hospital. I went there and I met Mr Abrahams, who is a consultant. As I was meeting him, the voices said to me, 'Tell him you have a tumour in your brain, and that you're in a lot of danger.' I said this to Mr Abrahams, but I know he didn't believe me. Anyway, he gave me a scan, and I did have a tumour.
I   What an incredible story? Did you have an operation?
A   Yes, I did. And after the operation, the voices came back again, and they said 'We're pleased we were able to help you. Goodbye.' And I've been in good health ever since. Now, what do you think of that?

T 12.6

1   A   Excuse me! Can I get past?
    B   Pardon?
    A   Can I get past, please?
    B   I'm sorry. I didn't hear you. Yes, of course.
    A   Thanks a lot.
2   A   I hear you're going to get married soon. Congratulations!
    B   That's right, next July. July 21. Can you come to the wedding?
    A   Oh, what a pity! That's when we're away

on holiday.

   C Never mind. We'll send you some wedding cake.

   A That's very kind.

3 **A** Oh, dear! Look at the time! Hurry up, or we'll miss the train.

   B Just a minute! I can't find my umbrella. Do you know where it is?

   A I haven't a clue. But you won't need it. It's a lovely day. Just look at the sky!

   B Oh, all right. Let's go, then.

4 **A** Good luck in your exam!

   B Same to you. I hope we both pass.

   A Did you go out last night?

   B No, of course not. I went to bed early. What about you?

   A Me, too. See you later, after the exam. Let's go out for a drink.

   B Good idea.

Unit 13

T 13.1

1 How long have you been sleeping on the streets?
For a year. It was very cold at first, but you get used to it.

2 Why did you come to London?
I came here to look for work, and I never left.

3 How long have you been selling *The Big Issue*?
For six months. I'm in Covent Garden seven days a week selling the magazine.

4 Have you made many friends?
Lots. But I can't stand people who think I drink or take drugs. My problem is I'm homeless. I want a job, but I need somewhere to live before I can get a job. So I need money to get somewhere to live, but I can't get money because I can't get a job, and I can't get a job because I haven't got somewhere to live. So I'm trapped.

5 How many copies do you sell a day?
Usually about fifty.

6 How many copies have you sold today?
So far, ten. But it's still early.

T 13.2

How long have you been trying to find a job?
How many jobs have you had?
How long have you been standing here today?
How did you lose your business?
How long have you had your dog?
Who's your best friend?
Where did you meet him?
How long have you known each other?

T 13.3

A How long have you been trying to find a job?

B For three years. It's been really difficult.

A How many jobs have you had?

B About thirty, maybe more. I've done everything.

A How long have you been standing here today?

B Since 8.00 this morning, and I'm freezing.

A How did you lose your business?

B I owed a lot of money in tax, and I couldn't pay it.

A How long have you had your dog?

B I've had her for about two months, that's all.

A Who's your best friend?

B A chap called Robbie, who's also from Scotland, like me.

A Where did you meet him?

B I met him here in London.

A How long have you known each other?

B About ten months. I met him soon after I came to London.

T 13.4 see T13.5

T 13.5 Phoning home

C = Craig   **M = His mother**

C Hi Mum. It's me, Craig.

M Craig! Hello! How lovely to hear from you. How are you? How's the new job going?

C Work's OK – I think. I'm just … so …

M Tired? You sound tired. Are you tired? What have you been doing?

C I *am* tired, really tired. I've been working so hard and everything's so new to me. I'm in the office until eight o'clock every night.

M Eight o'clock! Every night? That's terrible. And when do you eat? Have you been eating well?

C Yes, yes – I've been eating OK. After work, Tessa and I go out for a drink and something to eat in the pub round the corner. We're too tired to cook.

M Tessa? Who's Tessa?

C Tessa? Yes, Tessa. I'm sure I've told you about Tessa. We work together in the same office – she's been working here for a while, so she's been helping me a lot. She's really nice. You'd like her, Mum, if you met her. She lives near me.

M Mmm. Maybe you told your father about her, but not me. I've certainly never heard you talk about Tessa before.

C Ah yes. Dad. How is he? What's he been doing recently?

M Well, he's just returned from a business trip to Holland, so he hasn't been to work today, he's … he's been relaxing.

C Oh, yes of course. He's been working in Amsterdam, hasn't he? Well, I'm glad he's relaxing now. And what about you, Mum?

M Well, I was going to ring you actually. You see I'm coming to London next Tuesday. I'm going to a teachers' conference at the university, and I wondered if I could stay at your flat.

C Next Tuesday. That's great! Of course you can stay at my flat. I'll try to leave work earlier that day and I'll meet you after the conference. You can meet Tessa, too. We'll go out for a meal.

M Lovely! I'm looking forward to it already.

C Me too. See you next week. Bye for now. Love to Dad!

M Bye, Craig. Take care.

T 13.6 See p109

T 13.7

307 4922
1-800-878-5311
315 253 6031
517 592 2122
212 726 6390

T 13.8

P = Peter   **J = John**

1 **P** Hello. 793422.

   J Hello, Peter. This is John.

   P Hi, John. How are you?

   J Fine, thanks. And you?

   P All right. Did you have a nice weekend? You went away, didn't you?

   J Yes, we went to see some friends who live in the country. It was lovely. We had a good time.

   P Ah, good.

   J Peter, could you do me a favour? I'm playing squash tonight, but my racket's broken. Could I borrow yours?

   P Sure, that's fine.

   J Thanks a lot. I'll come and get it in half an hour, if that's OK.

   P Yes, I'll be in.

   J OK. Bye.

   P Bye.

A = Receptionist   **B = Student**
C = Ann, a teacher.

2 **A** Good morning. International School of English.

   B Hello, could I speak to Ann Baker, please?

   A Hold on. I'll connect you.

   C Hello.

   A Hello. Can I speak to Ann Baker, please?

   C Speaking.

   A Ah, hello. I saw your advertisement about English classes in a magazine. Could you send me some information, please?

   C Certainly. Can I just take some details? Could you give me your name and address, please?

A = Mike's flatmate   **B = Jim**

3 **A** Hello.

   B Hello. Is that Mike?

   A No, I'm afraid he's out at the moment. Can I take a message?

   B Yes, please. Can you say that Jim phoned, and I'll try again later. Do you know what time he'll be back?

   A In about an hour, I think.

   B Thanks. Goodbye.

   A Goodbye.

Unit 14

T 14.1 see p111

T 14.2 Listen and check

I was delighted because I'd passed all my exams.
I was hungry because I hadn't had any breakfast.
I went to bed early because I'd had a busy day.
Our teacher was angry because we hadn't done the homework.
My leg hurt because I'd fallen over playing football.
The plants died because I'd forgotten to water them.
The house was in a mess because we'd had a party the night before.

T 14.3 Which sentences contain *had*?

1 When we arrived she left.
2 When we arrived she'd left.
3 She'd like to leave now.
4 We'd stopped playing when the rain started.
5 We stopped playing when the rain started.

6 We'd play tennis if the rain stopped.
7 He checked that he'd turned off his mobile phone.
8 He turned off the television and went to bed.
9 I couldn't believe that I'd lost my passport again.
10 If I lost my passport, I'd be very upset.

T 14.4 What does Mary say?

I love John very much.
We met six months ago.
I've never been in love before.
We're very happy.
I'll love him forever.
I'm seeing him this evening.

T 14.5 What did Mary tell you?

Mary told me that she loved John very much. She said that they'd met six months ago and that she'd never been in love before. She told me that they were very happy and that she'd love him forever. She said that she was seeing him that evening.

T 14.6 An interview with Carmen Day

I = Interviewer   CD = Carmen Day

I   Carmen, why have you written another romantic novel?
CD Because I find romantic fiction easy to write, but my next novel won't be a romance. I'm hoping to write something different, perhaps a detective story.
I   In *One Short Hot Summer*, who is the character of Bradley based on?
CD Ah, well he's based on my first husband, Clive Maingay the actor. Clive made me very unhappy, very unhappy indeed.
I   You say 'your first husband' – have you then remarried?
CD Yes, indeed. I've been married for nearly ten years to Tony Marsh, you know, the politician.
I   Yes, I know him. Are you happy now?
CD Oh, yes. I can honestly say that I've found happiness again. Tony and I are very happy indeed.
I   Carmen, how many novels have you written so far?
CD Well, I've written five novels now, and three stories for children.
I   And when do you think you'll stop writing?
CD Never. I'll never stop. I'll continue to write even when I'm an old lady.

T 14.7

In an interview Carmen said she had written another romantic novel because she found romantic fiction easy to write, but that her next novel would be something different, possibly a detective story.

Carmen said that the character of Bradley was based on her first husband, Clive Maingay, the actor, who had made her very unhappy. But she added that she was now married to Tony Marsh, the politician. She said that they had been married for nearly ten years and that they were very happy together.

She told me that she had now written five novels, and also that she had written three stories for children. She said she would never stop writing, not even when she was an old lady.

T 14.8 A song

Talk to me

Well every night I see a light up in your window
But every night you won't answer the door
But although you won't ever let me in
From the street I can see your silhouette sitting close to him

What must I do?
What does it take
To get you to
Talk to me
Until the night is over
Talk to me
Well until the night is over, yeah yeah yeah
I got a full week's pay
And baby I've been working hard all day
I'm not asking for the world, you see
I'm just asking girl
Talk to me

Well late at night I hear music that you're playing soft and low
Yes and late at night I see the two of you swaying so close
I don't understand darling what was my sin?
Why am I down here below while you're up there with him?

What did I do?
What did I say?
What must I pay
To get you to
Talk to me
Until the night is over
Talk to me
Well until the night is over, yeah yeah yeah
I've got a full week's pay
And baby I've been working hard all day
I'm not asking for the world, you see
I'm just asking girl
Talk to me.

T 14.9 Saying goodbye

a Goodbye! Drive carefully and call us when you get there!
b Bye! See you later. Are you doing anything tonight?
c Goodbye! Have a safe journey. Send us a postcard!
d Goodbye. Here's my number. Please get in touch if you have any problems with it.
e Goodbye. It has been most interesting talking to you. We'll let you know by post.
f Goodbye! Good luck in the future. I've really enjoyed our lessons together!
g Bye-bye! Thank you for a lovely evening. You must come to us next time.
h Goodbye. Thank you for a lovely evening. You must come to us next time.

Grammar Reference

Unit 8

8.1 *have to*

Form

has/have + *to* + infinitive

Positive and negative

I We You They	have don't have		
		to	work hard.
He She It	has doesn't have		

Question

Do	I we you they	have to	work hard?
Does	he she it		

Short answer

Do you have to wear a uniform? Does he have to go now?	Yes, I do. No, he doesn't.

Note

1   The past tense of *have to* is *had to*, with *did* and *didn't* in the question and the negative.
   I **had to** get up early this morning.
   Why **did** you **have to** work last weekend?
   They liked the hotel because they **didn't have to** do any cooking.
2   The forms of *have got to* + infinitive are the same as *have got* + noun.

Use

1   *Have to* expresses strong obligation. The obligation comes from 'outside' – perhaps a law, a rule at school or work, or someone in authority.
   You **have to** have a driving licence if you want to drive a car. (That's the law.)
   I **have to** start work at 8.00. (My company says I must.)
   The doctor says I **have to** do more exercise.
2   *Don't/doesn't have to* expresses absence of obligation (it isn't necessary).
   You **don't have to** do the washing-up. I've got a dishwasher.
   She **doesn't have to** work on Monday. It's her day off.

8.2 Introduction to modal auxiliary verbs

Form

These are modal auxiliary verbs.

can   could   might   must
shall   should   will   would

They are looked at in different units of *Headway*.

They have certain things in common:
1   They 'help' another verb. The verb form is the infinitive without *to*.
   She **can** drive.
   I **must get** my hair cut.
2   There is no *do/does* in the question.
   Can she sing?
   Should I go home now?
3   The form is the same for all persons. There is no -*s* in the third person singular:
   He **can dance** very well.
   She **should try** harder.
   It **will rain** soon.
4   To form the negative, add *n't*. There is no *don't/doesn't*.
   I would**n't** like to be a teacher.
   You must**n't** steal.

   Note
   will not = *won't*.
   It **won't** rain tomorrow.
5   Most modal verbs refer to the present and future.
   Only *can* has a past tense form, *could*.
   I **could** swim when I was three.

8.3 *should*

Form

should + infinitive without *to*
The forms of *should* are the same for all persons.

Positive and negative

I He We They	should do more exercise. shouldn't tell lies.

Question

Should	I she they	see a doctor?	
Do you think		I he we	should see a doctor?

Short answer

Should I phone home? Should I buy a Mercedes Benz?	Yes, you should. No, you shouldn't.

Use

Should is used to express what the speaker thinks is right or the best thing to do. It expresses mild obligation, or advice.

> I **should** do more work. (This is my opinion.)
> You **should** do more work. (I'm telling you what I think.)
> Do you think we **should** stop here? (I'm asking you for your opinion.)

Shouldn't expresses negative advice.

> You **shouldn't** sit so close to the TV. It's bad for your eyes.

Note

Should expresses the opinion of the speaker, and it is often introduced by *I think* or *I don't think*.

> **I think** politicians **should** listen more.
> **I don't think** people **should** get married until they're 21.

8.4 *must*

Form

must + infinitive without *to*
The forms of *must* are the same for all persons.

Positive and negative

I He We They	must try harder. mustn't steal.

Questions with *must* are possible, but the use of *have to* is more common.

Question	Short answer
Must I take exams? Do I **have to** take exams?	Yes, you must. Yes, you do.

Use

1 *Must* expresses strong obligation. Generally, this obligation comes from 'inside' the speaker.
> I **must** get my hair cut. (I think this is necessary.)

2 Because *must* expresses the authority of the speaker, you should be careful of using *You must* … . It sounds very bossy!
> You **must** help me. (I am giving you an order.)
> *Could you help me?* is much better.

3 *You must* … can express a strong suggestion.
> **You must** see the Monet exhibition. It's wonderful.
> **You must** give me a ring when you're next in town.

Unit 9

9.1 Time clauses

1 Look at this sentence.
> *I'll give her a ring when I get home.*
> It consists of two clauses: a main clause *I'll give her a ring* and a secondary clause *when I get home*.

2 These conjunctions of time introduce secondary clauses.

when   while   as soon as   after   before   until

They are not usually followed by a future form. They refer to future time, but we use a present tense.

> **When** I get home, I'll …
> **While** we're away, …
> **As soon as** I hear from you, …
> Wait here **until** I get back.

9.2 *will*

Form

For the forms of *will*, see Part A p73.

Use

1 *Will* expresses a decision or intention made at the moment of speaking.
> Give me your case. **I'll** carry it for you.

2 It also expresses a future fact. The speaker thinks 'This action is sure to happen in the future'.
> Manchester **will** win the cup.
> Tomorrow's weather **will** be warm and sunny.

This use is like a neutral future tense. The speaker is predicting the future, without expressing an intention, plan, or personal judgement.

9.3 First conditional

Form

if + Present Simple, *will* + infinitive without *to*

Positive and negative

If	I work hard, I she has enough money, she we don't hurry up, we you're late, I	'll (will) won't	pass my exams. buy a new car. be late. wait for you.

Question

What Where	will	you do she go	if	you don't go to university? she can't find a job?

Short answer

Will you go to university if you pass your exams?	Yes, I will. No, I won't.
If we look after the planet, will we survive?	Yes, we will. No, we won't.

Note

The condition clause *if* … can come at the beginning of the sentence or at the end. If it comes at the begining, we put a comma at the end of the clause. If it comes at the end, we do not use a comma.

> **If** I work hard**,** I'll pass my exams.
> I'll pass my exams **if** I work hard.

Use

1 The first conditional is used to express a possible condition and a probable result in the future.
> **If** my cheque **comes**, **I'll buy** us all a meal.
> You**'ll get** wet if you **don't take** an umbrella.
> What**'ll happen** to the environment if we **don't look after** it?

Note

1 English uses a present tense in the condition clause, not a future form.
> If it **rains** …   NOT   If it ~~will rain~~ …
> If I **work** hard …   NOT   If ~~I'll work~~ hard …

2 *If* expresses a possibility that something will happen; *when* expresses what the speaker sees as certain to happen.
> **If** I find your book, I'll send it to you.
> **When** I get home, I'll have a bath.

Unit 10

10.1 Verb patterns 2

Verb patterns were first covered in Unit 5 Part A. There is a list of verb patterns on p130.

1 Verb + *to* + infinitive
   They **managed to escape**.
   I **try to visit** somewhere new.
   We **decided to go** abroad.
2 *go* + *-ing* for sports and activities
   Let's **go skiing**.
   We **went dancing**.
3 Verb + sb + infinitive without *to*
   My teachers **made** me **work** hard.
   My parents **let** me **go out** when I want.

10.2 *used to*

Form

used + *to* + infinitive
Used to is the same in all persons.

Positive and negative

I She We They	used to didn't use to	smoke. like cooking.

Question

What did you use to do?

Short answer

Did you use to smoke a lot?	Yes, I did./No, I didn't.

Note

1 The question form is not often used. We ask a question in the Past Simple, and reply using *used to*.
   Where **did** you **go** on holiday when you were young?
   We **used to go** camping in France.
2 *Never* is often used.
   I **never** used to watch TV.
3 Be careful not to confuse *to use* (e.g. *I **use** a knife to cut an apple.*) and *used to*.
   The pronunciation is also different.
   to use /juːz/   used to /juːstuː/ or /juːstə/

Use

Used to is used:
1 to express a past habit.
   He **used to** play football every Saturday, but now he doesn't.
2 to express a past state.
   They **used to** be happy together, but now they fight all the time.

10.3 *used to* and the Past Simple

1 The Past Simple can also be used to express a past habit or state.
   He **played** football every Sunday when he **was** a boy.
   They **were** happy together when they **were** first married.
2 Only the Past Simple can be used for actions which happened once in the past.
   We used to go to France every summer, but once, in 1987, we **went** to Greece.
   Last night I **drank** champagne.

Note

Used to has no equivalent in the present. The Present Simple is used for present habits and states.
   She **lives** in New York.
   She sometimes **comes** to London on business.

10.4 Infinitives

1 Infinitives are used to express purpose. They answer the question *Why … ?* This use is very common in English.
   I'm learning English **to get** a good job.
   She's saving her money **to buy** a car.
   I'm going to Scotland **to visit** my parents.

Note

Some languages express this idea of purpose with a translation of *for* + infinitive. English does not use *for*.
   I came here **to learn** English.
   NOT   I came here ~~for to~~ learn English.
          I came here ~~for~~ learn English.
2 Infinitives are used after certain adjectives.

I'm	pleased surprised	to see you.
It's	hard important impossible	to learn Chinese.

3 Infinitives are used after the question words *who, what, where, how,* etc.
   Can you tell me **how to get** to the station?
   I don't know **who to speak** to.
   Show me **what to do**.
4 Infinitives are used after the compounds *something, nothing, nowhere, anybody,* etc.
   Have **something to eat**!
   I've got **nothing to do**.
   There's **nowhere to hide**.
   Is there **anyone to talk** to?

Unit 11

11.1 The passive

Form

$$\left.\begin{array}{l} \textit{am/is/are} \\ \textit{was/were} \\ \textit{has/have been} \\ \textit{will be} \end{array}\right\} + \textit{-ed} \text{ (past participle)}$$

The past participle of regular verbs ends in *-ed*. There are many common irregular verbs. See the list on p130.

Present

Positive and negative

English **is spoken** all over the world.
Renault cars **are made** in France.
My children **aren't helped** with their homework.
Coffee **isn't grown** in England.

Question

Where **is** rice **grown**?
Are cars **made** in your country?

Past

Positive and negative

My car **was stolen** last night.
The animals **were frightened** by a loud noise.
He **wasn't injured** in the accident.
The thieves **weren't seen** by anyone.

Question

How **was** the window **broken**?
Were the plants **watered** last night?

Present Perfect

Positive and negative

I've **been robbed**!
Diet Coke **has been made** since 1982.
They **haven't been invited** to the party.

Question

How many times **have** you **been hurt** playing football?
Has my car **been repaired**?

will

Positive and negative

10,000 cars **will be produced** next year.
The cars **won't be sold** in the UK.

Question

Will the children **be sent** to a new school?

Short answer

Are cars made in your country?	Yes, they are./No, they aren't.
Were the plants watered last night?	Yes, they were./No, they weren't.
Has my car been repaired?	Yes, it has./No, it hasn't.
Will these cars be produced next year?	Yes, they will./No, they won't.

Note

1   The rules for tense usage in the passive are the same as in the active.
Present Simple to express habit:
My car **is serviced** regularly.
Past Simple to express a finished action in the past:
America **was discovered** by Christopher Columbus.
Present Perfect to express an action which began in the past and continues to the present:
Diet Coke **has been made** since 1982.

2   The passive infinitive (*to be* + *-ed*) is used after modal auxiliary verbs and other verbs which are followed by an infinitive.
Driving should **be banned** in city centres.
The house is going **to be knocked down**.

Use

1   The object of an active verb becomes the subject of a passive verb. Notice the use of *by* in the passive sentence.

Object

Active   Shakespeare wrote *Hamlet*.

Passive   *Hamlet* was written by Shakespeare.

Subject

2   The passive is not another way of expressing the same sentence in the active. We choose the active or the passive depending on what we are more interested in.
Hamlet **was written** in 1600. (We are more interested in *Hamlet*.)
Shakespeare **wrote** comedies, histories, and tragedies. (We are more interested in Shakespeare.)

Note

Some verbs, for example, *give, send, show*, have two objects, a person and a thing.
She **gave me** a **book** for my birthday.
In the passive, we often make the person the subject, not the thing.
I was given a book for my birthday.
She was sent the information by post.
You'll be shown where to sit.

Unit 12

12.1 Second conditional

Form

if + Past Simple, *would* + infinitive without *to*
Would is a modal auxiliary verb. There is an introduction to modal auxiliary verbs on p124.
The forms of *would* are the same for all persons.

Positive and negative

If	I had more money, I she knew the answer, she we lived in Russia, we I didn't have so many debts, I	'd (would) wouldn't	buy a CD player. tell us. soon learn Russian. have to work so hard.

Question

What Which countries	would	you do you go to	if	you had a year off? you travelled round the world?

Short answer

Would you travel round the world? If they had the money, would they buy a new car?	Yes, I would./No, I wouldn't. Yes, they would./No, they wouldn't.

Note

1 The condition clause can come at the beginning or the end of the sentence. If it comes at the beginning, we put a comma at the end of the clause. If it comes at the end, we do not use a comma.
   If I had more time, **I'd** help.
   I'd help **if** I had more time.
2 *Were* is often used instead of *was* in the condition clause.
   If I **were** you, I'd go to bed.
   If he **were** cleverer, he'd know he was making a mistake.

Use

The second conditional is used to express and unreal or improbable condition and its probable result in the present or future.
The condition is unreal because it is different from the facts that we know. We can always say 'But … '.
   If I were Prime Minister, **I'd increase** tax for rich people. (But I'm not Prime Minister.)
   If I lived in a big house, **I'd have** a party. (But I live in a small house.)
   What **would** you **do if you saw** a ghost? (But I don't expect that you will see a ghost.)

Note

1 The use of the past tense (If I had) and *would* does not refer to past time. Both the first and second conditional refer to the present and the future. The past verb forms are used to show 'This is different from reality'.
   If I win the tennis match, **I'll be** happy. (I think I have a good chance.)
   If I won a thousand pounds, **I'd …** (But I don't think I will.)
2 We do not use *would* in the condition clause.
   If the weather **was** nice …   NOT If the weather ~~would be~~ nice …
   If I **had** more money …   NOT If I ~~would have~~ more money …

12.2 *might*

Form

might + infinitive without *to*
Might is a modal auxiliary verb. For an introduction to modal auxiliary verbs, see p124.
The forms of *might* are the same for all persons.

Positive and negative

I He It We	might might not	go to the party. be late. rain tomorrow. go out for a meal tonight.

Question

The inverted question *Might you … ?* is unusual. It is very common to ask a question with *Do you think … + will … ?*

Do you think	you'll get here on time? it'll rain? they'll come to our party?

Short answer

Do you think he'll come? Do you think it'll rain?	He might. It might.

Use

1 *Might* is used to express a future possibility. It contrasts with *will*, which, in the speaker's opinion, expresses a future certainty.
   England **will** win the match.
   (I am sure they will.)
   England **might** win the match.
   (It's possible, but I don't know.)
2 Notice that, in the negative, these sentences express the same idea of possibility.
   It **might not** rain this afternoon.
   I **don't think it'll** rain this afternoon.

Unit 13

13.1 Present Perfect Continuous

Form

has/have + *been* + *-ing* (present participle)

Positive and negative

I We You They	've (have) haven't	been working.
He She It	's (has) hasn't	

Question

How long	have	I we you they	been working?
	has	he she it	

Short answer

Have you been running? Has he been shopping?	Yes, I have./No, I haven't. Yes, he has./No, he hasn't.

Use

The Present Perfect Continuous is used:
1 to express an activity which began in the past and continues to the present.
> We've been waiting here for hours!
> It's been raining for days.
2 to refer to an activity with a result in the present.
> I'm hot because I've been running.
> I haven't got any money because I've been shopping.

Note

1 Sometimes there is little or no difference in meaning between the Present Perfect Simple and Continuous.
> How long have you worked here?
> How long have you been working here?
2 Think of the verbs that have the idea of a long time, for example, *wait, work, learn, travel, play.*
These verbs can be found in the Present Perfect Continuous.
> I've been playing tennis since I was a boy.
Think of the verbs that don't have the idea of a long time, for example, *find, start, buy, die, lose, break, stop*. It is unusual to find these verbs in the Present Perfect Continuous.
> I've bought a new dress.
> My cat has died.
> My radio's broken.
3 Verbs that express a state, for example, *like, love, know, have* for possession, are not found in the Present Perfect Continuous.
> We've known each other for a few weeks.
> NOT   We've ~~been knowing~~ each other for a few weeks.
> How long have you had your car?
> NOT   How long have you ~~been having~~ your car?
4 The Present Perfect Simple looks at the completed action. This is why, if the sentence gives a number or a quantity, the Present Perfect Simple is used. The Continuous is not possible.
> I've written three letters today.
> NOT   I've ~~been writing~~ three letters today.

Unit 14

14.1 Past Perfect

Form

had + *-ed* (past participle)
The past participle of regular verbs ends in *-ed*. There are many common irregular verbs. See the list on p130.

Positive and negative

I He/She/It We/You/They	'd (had) hadn't	arrived before 10.00.

Question

Had	I he/she/it we/you/they	left?

Short answer

Yes, he had. No, they hadn't.

Use

The Past Perfect is used to express an action in the past which happened before another action in the past.

Action 2   Action 1

When I got home, John **had cooked** a meal.

Note

Notice the use of the Past Perfect and the Past Simple in the following sentences.
> When I got home, John **cooked** a meal. (First I got home, then John cooked.)
> When I got home, John **had cooked** a meal. (John cooked a meal before I got home.)

14.2 Reported statements

Form

The usual rule is that the verb form moves 'one tense back'.

Direct speech	Reported speech
Present	**Past**
'I love you.'	He said he loved me.
'I'm going out now.'	Ann said she was going out.
Present Perfect	**Past Perfect**
'We've met before.'	She said they'd met before.
Past Simple	**Past Perfect**
'We met in 1987.'	He said they'd met in 1987.
will	**would**
'I'll mend it for you.'	She said that she would mend it for me.
can	**could**
'I can swim.'	She said she could swim.

Note

Notice the use of *say/tell*.
Say + (that)
> She **said** (that) they were happy together.
Tell + person (that)
> He **told me** (that) he loved Mary.

Appendix 1

IRREGULAR VERBS

Base form	Past Simple	Past Participle
be	was/were	been
become	became	become
begin	began	begun
break	broke	broken
bring	brought	brought
build	built	built
buy	bought	bought
can	could	been able
catch	caught	caught
choose	chose	chosen
come	came	come
cost	cost	cost
cut	cut	cut
do	did	done
drink	drank	drunk
drive	drove	driven
eat	ate	eaten
fall	fell	fallen
feel	felt	felt
fight	fought	fought
find	found	found
fly	flew	flown
forget	forgot	forgotten
get	got	got
give	gave	given
go	went	gone/been
grow	grew	grown
have	had	had
hear	heard	heard
hit	hit	hit
keep	kept	kept
know	knew	known
learn	learnt/learned	learnt/learned
leave	left	left
lose	lost	lost
make	made	made
meet	met	met
pay	paid	paid
put	put	put
read /ri:d/	read /red/	read /red/
ride	rode	ridden
run	ran	run
say	said	said
see	saw	seen
sell	sold	sold
send	sent	sent
shut	shut	shut
sing	sang	sung
sit	sat	sat
sleep	slept	slept
speak	spoke	spoken
spend	spent	spent
stand	stood	stood
steal	stole	stolen
swim	swam	swum
take	took	taken
tell	told	told
think	thought	thought
understand	understood	understood
wake	woke	woken
wear	wore	worn
win	won	won
write	wrote	written

Appendix 2

VERB PATTERNS

Verb + *-ing*	
like	
love	swimming
enjoy	
hate	cooking
finish	
stop	

Note

We often use the verb *go* + *-ing* for sports and activities.

    I **go swimming** everyday.

    I **go shopping** at the weekend.

Verb + *to* + infinitive	
choose	
decide	
forget	
promise	
manage	to go
need	
help	
hope	
try	to work
want	
would like	
would love	

Verb + *-ing* or *to* + infinitive	
begin	raining/to rain
start	

Verb + sb + infinitive without *to*		
let	somebody	go
make		do

Modal auxiliary verbs	
can	
could	
shall	go
will	
would	arrive

Phonetic symbols

Consonants

1	/p/	as in	**pen** /pen/
2	/b/	as in	**big** /bɪg/
3	/t/	as in	**tea** /tiː/
4	/d/	as in	**do** /duː/
5	/k/	as in	**cat** /kæt/
6	/g/	as in	**go** /gəʊ/
7	/f/	as in	**four** /fɔː/
8	/v/	as in	**very** /ˈveri/
9	/s/	as in	**son** /sʌn/
10	/z/	as in	**zoo** /zuː/
11	/l/	as in	**live** /lɪv/
12	/m/	as in	**my** /maɪ/
13	/n/	as in	**near** /nɪə/
14	/h/	as in	**happy** /ˈhæpi/
15	/r/	as in	**red** /red/
16	/j/	as in	**yes** /jes/
17	/w/	as in	**want** /wɒnt/
18	/θ/	as in	**thanks** /θæŋks/
19	/ð/	as in	**the** /ðə/
20	/ʃ/	as in	**she** /ʃiː/
21	/ʒ/	as in	**television** /ˈtelɪvɪʒn/
22	/tʃ/	as in	**child** /tʃaɪld/
23	/dʒ/	as in	**German** /ˈdʒɜːmən/
24	/ŋ/	as in	**English** /ˈɪŋglɪʃ/

Vowels

25	/iː/	as in	**see** /siː/
26	/ɪ/	as in	**his** /hɪz/
27	/i/	as in	**twenty** /ˈtwenti/
28	/e/	as in	**ten** /ten/
29	/æ/	as in	**stamp** /stæmp/
30	/ɑː/	as in	**father** /ˈfɑːðə/
31	/ɒ/	as in	**hot** /hɒt/
32	/ɔː/	as in	**morning** /ˈmɔːnɪŋ/
33	/ʊ/	as in	**football** /ˈfʊtbɔːl/
34	/uː/	as in	**you** /juː/
35	/ʌ/	as in	**sun** /sʌn/
36	/ɜː/	as in	**learn** /lɜːn/
37	/ə/	as in	**letter** /ˈletə/

Diphthongs (two vowels together)

38	/eɪ/	as in	**name** /neɪm/
39	/əʊ/	as in	**no** /nəʊ/
40	/aɪ/	as in	**my** /maɪ/
41	/aʊ/	as in	**how** /haʊ/
42	/ɔɪ/	as in	**boy** /bɔɪ/
43	/ɪə/	as in	**hear** /hɪə/
44	/eə/	as in	**where** /weə/
45	/ʊə/	as in	**tour** /tʊə/

OXFORD
UNIVERSITY PRESS

Great Clarendon Street, Oxford OX2 6DP

Oxford University Press is a department of the University of Oxford. It furthers the University's objective of excellence in research, scholarship, and education by publishing worldwide in

Oxford New York

Auckland Cape Town Dar es Salaam Hong Kong Karachi Kuala Lumpur Madrid Melbourne Mexico City Nairobi New Delhi Shanghai Taipei Toronto

With offices in

Argentina Austria Brazil Chile Czech Republic France Greece Guatemala Hungary Italy Japan Poland Portugal Singapore South Korea Switzerland Thailand Turkey Ukraine Vietnam

OXFORD and OXFORD ENGLISH are registered trade marks of Oxford University Press in the UK and in certain other countries

© Oxford University Press 2000

The moral rights of the author have been asserted

Database right Oxford University Press (maker)

First published 2000

2009 2008 2007

10 9 8 7

ISBN-13: 978 0 19 436670 0 (Complete Edition)

ISBN-13: 978 0 19 437879 6 (Student's Book A)

ISBN-13: 978 0 19 437880 2 (Student's Book B)

Printed China

ACKNOWLEDGEMENTS

The authors and publisher are grateful to those who have given permission to reproduce the following extracts and adaptations of copyright material:

p22 'The burglars' friend' *The Daily Mail* 5 February 1996 © *The Daily Mail*/Solo Syndication.

p34 'The best shopping street in the world' by Anne Applebaum, *The London Evening Standard* 27 October 1998 © *The London Evening Standard*/Solo Syndication.

p42 'The kids from fame' by Carrie Fisher, *Observer Life Magazine* 13 April 1997 © *The Observer*.

p44 *You've Got a Friend* Words and music by Carole King © 1971 Screen Gems-EMI Music Ltd, London WC2H 0EA. Reproduced by permission of IMP Ltd.

p50 'The man who gave his money away' by Tony Burton, *Mail Weekend Magazine* 31 December 1994 © *The Daily Mail Weekend Magazine*/Solo Syndication

p51 'Hetty Green' from *Virtual Vermont Internet Magazine* www.virtualvermont.com Reproduced by permission of *Virtual Vermont Internet Magazine.*

p73 'Future tense? No, the future will be perfect' interview with Michio Kaku, *Focus Magazine* October 1998. Reproduced by permission of Michio Kaku.

p74 'One day all this will be offices' by Jonathon Glancey, *The Guardian* 11 July 1998 © *The Guardian.*

p78 'All alone with my rocky horrors' by Paul Lay, *The Telegraph* 3 October 1998 reproduced by permission of Paul Lay.

p82 'Into the wild' by Jon Krakauer, published by Macmillan Publishers Ltd, reproduced by permission of John A Ware Literary Agency.

p99 'Reverend ghostbuster faces another haunting hallowe'en' by Martin Wroe, *The Observer* 26 October 1997 © *The Observer*.

p106 'Tom, 69, skates on for Tesco' *The Daily Mail* 18 February 1999 © *The Daily Mail*/Solo Syndication.

p107 'Life's a beach patrol' by Cordell Marks, *The Weekend Telegraph* September 9 1995 reproduced by permission of Cordell Marks.

p114 'The tale of two silent brothers' from Oxford Bookworms: *Stories From The Five Towns*. Reproduced by permission of Jennifer Bassett.

p116 *Talk to me* by Bruce Springsteen. Copyright © Bruce Springsteen (ASCAP) Administered by Zomba Music Publishers Ltd. In UK & Eire Only. Reproduced by permission of Zomba Music Publishers Ltd.

Although every effort has been made to trace and contact copyright holders before publication, this has not been possible in some cases. We apologize for any apparent infringement of copyright and if notified, the publisher will be pleased to rectify any errors or omissions at the earliest opportunity.

p26 'The Perfect Crime' This story is based on Roald Dahl's *Lamb to the Slaughter* but was written without the knowledge or approval of the Dahl estate. The publishers apologize to the Estate for this oversight and are grateful to the Estate for their understanding in allowing them to include the story nevertheless. You can read Roald Dahl's original story in his short story collection *Someone Like You*, published by Penguin Books.

Illustrations by:

Kathy Baxendale p30 (list), 108 (diary writing); CartoonStock/Larry p24; Rowie Christopher pp56, 61, 116; Martin Cottam pp114, 115; Paul Dickinson p111; Jessie Eckel, New Division p32; Tim Kahane p14; Ian Kellas pp12, 20, 21, 28, 40, 52, 71, 85, 100; Beverly Levy pp110, 111, 112; Gone Loco, Debut Art p29; Mark Olroyd p84; Pierre Paul Pariseau pp25, 68; Andy Parker p26; Oxford University Press TechGraphics pp74, 79; Debbie Ryder p53; Harry Venning pp10, 60, 64, 69, 72, 78, 96, 104; Azélie Williams pp94, 95

Commissioned photography by:

Gareth Boden pp6, 7, 21, 37, 38, 58–9, 66, 69, 70, 72, 93 (out of order, this room is ready, engaged), 94, 96–7, 101, 103, 108, 117 Haddon Davies pp12, 30 Mark Mason pp9, 26–7, 30, 36, 54–5, 73 (Visions), 90, 93 (under 18), 108

photo 58–9:

Location: Mr and Mrs M Stewart, Wytham Abbey, Oxford
Hair by Seed, Oxford
Make-up by Sarah Heap, The Make-up Place
Clothes from Allders of Oxford
Glasses from Boots the Optician

Locations provided by:

Gareth Boden pp101 (entrance hallway), 108 (living room)

Boots p37 (chemist); Café Rouge, Hertford p37 (café); Censored p37 (clothes shop), Countryside Residential Properties pp7, 108 (kitchen), 117 (exterior of house & entrance hallway); Goldsmiths p101 (jewellers); Harlow College p96–7; Antonia Jack pp38, 72, 117 (kitchen & birthday); Post Office Counters p37 (post office); Studio Cambridge pp21, 101 (school), 117 (classroom); Thaxted Surgery p69; WAGN p117 (train station); Waitrose p101 (supermarket)

We would also like to thank the following for permission to reproduce photographs:

The Advertising Archives pp87 (1908 Coke advertisement), 92 (Wrigley's pixie at bottom), (girl with pixies), (women in white hats); *AKG London* p87 (sailor girl), 90 (tobacco), (cotton); *The Ancient Art & Architecture Collection* pp11 (Greek theatre masks); *The Art Archive* pp11 (Archaeological Museum, Naples/man reading scroll), (Egyptian Museum, Cairo/ Egyptian papyrus); *The Anthony Blake Photo Library* pp65 (fondue), (A Sydenham/Mexican food), (G Buntrock/mint tea); *The Bridgeman Art Library* p90 (Royal Asiatic Society/sugar cane); *Bubbles Photo Library* pp8 (F Rombout/family by river), 17 (L Tizard), 107 (J Woodcock/ Cathy); *J Allan Cash* p93 (feeding of animals, one way); *Anthony Coleman* p107 (Terry Cemm *both*); *Collections* pp38 (B Shuel/ Justin), 93 (B Wells/keep off the grass); *Colorific!* pp14 (T Graham/Maori), (B Backman/sheep), 49 (J Tove Johansson/cottage), 51 (C Bernson/Milton Petrie); *Comstock* pp63 (all); *Corbis* pp6 (S Maze/Bologna), 10 (R Holmes/conversation), 16 (B Krist/barbecue), 20 (D Modricker/COR/older couple), 45 (Picture Press/man at desk), (Wartenberg/Picture Press/man smiling), 47 (C Osborne/Melbourne), 51 (Bettmann/Hetty Green *both*), 66 (D Katzenstein), 80 (D Gluckstein/middle-aged man), 81 (B Varie/man in office), (F Wartenberg/couple with gift), (L Manning/girl on steps), (Bettmann/man and pipe), (C Garratt/Milepost 92?/security notice); *Corbis Sygma* pp42–3 (L Greenfield/poster), 74 (J van Hasselt/poster); *Digital Vision* p19 (New York); *Fortean Picture Library* p98 (J & C Bord/ghost); *Agencja Gazeta*, Warsaw pp34, 35 (M Mutor); *Getty One Stone* pp10 (W Kaehler/monkeys), 13 (K Fisher/mother and child), (PBJ Pictures/college students), (PBJ Pictures/business people), 15 (L Adamski Peek/ice hockey), (D Madison/ football), (D Balfour/giraffe), 16 (A Sacks/girls hairstyling), 18 (Rohan), 19 (D Durfee/Roberto Solano), (S Cohen/ Yuet Tung), 20 (B Thomas/young couple), 23 (F Alison), 38 (P Cade/Sean), (M Douet/Martyn), 39 (T Reynolds/ Mel), 45 (I O'Leary/ill woman), (L Monneret/girl with presents), (R E Daemrich/yawning boy), 46 (B Thomas), 47 (R La Salle/Chicago), (D Armand/Dubai), (H Pfeiffer/ Paris), 48 (S Grandadam/Stockholm, Brazilia), 49 (C Ehlers/girls fishing), 57 (H Camille/Guy and Suzie), 65 (R Elliot/Alpine restaurant), (R During/Acapulco beach), 81 (D Day/woman and spider), (D Stewart/man and knife), (C Slattery/rollercoaster), 84 (P Lee Harvey/man), 107 (D Ham/balloon), 109 (L Dutton), 113 (L Monneret); *Sally & Richard Greenhill* pp13 (elderly couple talking); *Robert Harding Picture Library* pp19 (© Noble Stock/ Int'l Stock/Endre Boros), 49 (midnight sun), 76 (N Boyd/ hotel exterior), (F Jalain/swimming pool), (P Langone/ Int'l Stock/conference room and bar), (D Dickinson/Int'l Stock/gym), 93 (S Harris/train departures); *Hulton Getty* pp54 (Anthony Trollope), 80 (boy), 91 (Office of Information for Puerto Rico/sugar cane), (Evans/woman and cotton), 92 (Reiss/American soldiers), (Wrigley's pixie at top); *The Image Bank* pp13 (M Romanelli/men talking in café), 62 (R Mancini), 65 (G A Rossi/market stall); *Images Colour Library* pp82–3 (Panoramic Images); *Impact Photos* p93 (S Shepheard/Undergound); *The Kobal Collection* pp104 (TM & © 1993 Universal City Studios and Amblin Entertainment. All Rights Reserved/ *Schindler's List*), 105 (Lucasfilm/Paramount '81/ *Raiders of the Lost Ark*), (David James 1998 TM & Dreamworks LLC Paramount Pictures Amblin Entertainment. All Rights Reserved/*Saving Private Ryan*), (Warner Bros/Steven Spielberg); *Magnum Photos* pp74 (I Berry/Shenzen building site), 75 (Hong Kong cityscape); *Oxford Picture Library* p33; Oxford University Press p73 (Michio Kaku); *PhotoDisc* p41; *Photofusion* p45 (M Campbell/woman in car), 98 (B Apicella/woman); *Photographers International* p99 (T Fincher); *Pictorial Press* pp104 (Columbia/*Close Encounters of the Third Kind*), 105 (UPI/ *Jurassic Park*); *Redferns* pp57 (M Hutson/concert); *Ringway Signs Ltd* p93 (services); *Science Photo Library* pp10 (M Agliolo/computer screens), (D Ducros/satellite), 73 (A Pasieka/DNA fingerprinting *background*), (P Plailly/ boy and hologram), (B Edmaier/lava); *John & Liz Soars* p8 (Joy Darling); *Solo Syndication* p106 (Frank Spooner Pictures p50 (Jordan/Gamma), 55 (P Massey/ Joanna Trollope), 86 (N Reynard/Kenyan man drinking), 87 (G Fonluft/Coke bottles), 88 (A Hernandez-Liaison/ MacDonalds); *Still Pictures* p73 (H Schwarzbach/solar panels in Sudan); *The Stock Market* pp38 (A Skelley/ Amy), 48 (D Croucher/Paris), 73 (Zefa/medical scanner); *Stock Shot* p79 (O Willis/El Chorro Gorge); *The Telegraph* p78 (P Lay/Paul Lay); *Telegraph Colour Library* pp8 (R Gage/family portrait), 10 (J Danielsky/ mobile phone), (F Delva/film), 24 (R Chapple/Zoe), (S Miller/police detective), 44 (J P Fruchet), 48 (T Chevassut/ Beijing), 65 (S Adams/snowboarding), (P Scholey/Nile cruise), (K Ross/pyramids), 88 (hamburger); *Tesco Photo Library* p93 (unleaded)